FOREWORD BY GENERAL MICHAEL T. FLYNN

PATRICK BYRNE

DANGER CLOSE

Domestic Extremist #1
Comes Clean

PREFACE BY MARIA BUTINA

Danger Close: Domestic Extremist #1 Comes Clean

First Edition: 2024

Printed in the United States of America

10 9 8 7 6 5 4 3 2 1

This book is a work of non-fiction. The author has made every effort to ensure that the accuracy of the information in this book was correct at time of publication. Neither the author nor the publisher nor any other person(s) associated with this book may be held liable for any damages that may result from any of the ideas made by the author in this book.

ISBN-13: 978-1-963102-10-9 (Paperback)
ISBN-13: 978-1-963102-11-6 (Hardcover)
ISBN-13: 978-1-963102-09-3 (eBook)

Disclaimer: The author of this book is solely responsible for the accuracy and truthfulness of the content. The publisher does not endorse, verify, or assume responsibility for any statements made within the book, including any potentially defamatory or false claims. Any legal responsibility related to the content lies with the author, and the publisher disclaims any liability for the same.

Cover design by TLC Book Design, TLCBookDesign.com
Published by Defiance Press and Publishing, LLC

Bulk orders of this book may be obtained by contacting Defiance Press and Publishing, LLC. www.defiancepress.com.

Public Relations Dept. – Defiance Press & Publishing, LLC
281-581-9300
pr@defiancepress.com

Defiance Press & Publishing, LLC
281-581-9300
info@defiancepress.com

To my mother, Dorothy M. Byrne, who drew me this way.

TABLE OF CONTENTS

PROLOGUE

BY GENERAL MICHAEL T. FLYNN

Through my work as a senior intelligence officer in the world of national security and special operations, I have known about the courageous work Patrick Byrne has been directed to do on behalf of the United States Government. Most people don't understand the work of "national intelligence assets," but that is what Patrick has been asked to be within the opaque world of government-to-government relationships. He's been placed into extremely difficult positions and has had to use his judgment to accomplish his directed missions to the best of his ability.

This takes extraordinary judgment and courage. I've gotten to personally know Patrick over the past few years because of his USG directed role in rooting out corruption. He has been unshakable when it comes to his relentless pursuit of exposing the deep levels of corruption within our government. For a man who thought his life would be spent engaging an overseas adversary, he found himself battling his own government.

The incredible story of bribery, blackmail, rape, murder, and other tales—normally the stuff found in novels—are the truth coming from a man who was asked to enable, encourage, or conduct these actions on behalf of our very own government. Patrick's story is for real, he's for real, the corruption he's exposed is for real, and it only gets worse the further you read.

General Michael T. Flynn (ret.)
July 2023
Sarasota, Florida

PREFACE

BY MARIA BUTINA

Prisoner #374794
US Bureau of Prisons

In the nineteenth century, the expression "The emperor has no clothes" was firmly planted in the world's lexicon thanks to the children's morality tale by Danish writer Hans Christian Andersen. Since then, it has come to be used in the context of the uncertainty that a person feels attempting to criticize someone or something that is highly regarded and supported by the masses.

Over the course of two centuries, the expression's usage has expanded to more than one hundred languages of the world. And despite its considerable age, its use is more relevant than ever, as today's society seems less able than ever to process critically the information given to it.

Fortunately, not everything is lost. The braves, the lone wolves continue to emerge, men and women courageous enough to tell the truth despite the crowd's blindness.

Now in modern America such a fearless knight is Patrick Byrne.

The Fate brought us together on a sad occasion—the American government decided to set me up then scapegoat me for so-called "Russian

Collusion" with Trump's presidential campaign (collusion which was non-existent, as both the Durham and Mueller reports later confirmed). I ended up in an American prison for eighteen months.

To my deep regret, Patrick was directly related to this, as he became "patient zero" in the Maria Butina case working for the FBI against me.

However, when Patrick figured out what was happening behind the scenes and how both he and I were simply being used in Barack Obama's political games, he went public and told the truth about his role in this case, and the dirty games of the American deep state.

Patrick lost everything: the truth cost him the company he created, a huge media campaign was launched against him, he was threatened with criminal prosecution. But Patrick has pressed on. Just as he did once at other times in his life, such as when he exposed the truth about the Wall Street corruption, and more recently, the fraud of the 2020 US presidential election.

He doesn't give up. He just keeps going. Just as he is doing now.

Patrick Byrne is the man who in today's America who is not afraid to say, "The Emperor has no clothes."

This is worthy of respect.

During those rare times we had together, Patrick and I spent hours and hours talking. I have translated his articles and books into Russian. And as a Russian I can say for sure that, although Patrick isn't Russian by nationality, he has the depth of soul of a Russian.

Maria Valerievna Butina
November 2023
Moscow, Russia

INTRODUCTION

"WALL STREET GOLDEN BOY" TO "DOMESTIC EXTREMIST THREAT #1"

"These days, when people talk of Byrne, the word 'vindication' comes up a lot," opened an article in the *Salt Lake Tribune* as the financial system quaked into crisis in August 2008.

Not long after that, financial journalist Charles Gasparino scolded his CNBC cohosts on-air for how they had endlessly attacked Byrne from 2005-2008 regarding claims about which he had turned out to be correct: "Patrick Byrne was right, all along…the Overstock guy…that everybody made fun of…" rebuked Gasparino to a shame-faced Jim Cramer and Becky Quick.

Months later, the *Wall Street Journal* included Byrne in its year-end list ("2008 Look back: Best Calls of the Year") of five people who deserved credit for seeing the financial crisis coming (others included Jamie Dimon, Nassim Taleb, and Nouriel Roubini).

In October 2008, Alan Greenspan explained to Congress the origins of the financial collapse, and gave testimony that became famous:

Dr. Alan Greenspan,
October 23, 2008

There are additional regulatory changes that this breakdown of the central pillar of competitive markets requires in order to return to stability, particularly in the areas of fraud, settlement, and securitization.

"By 'fraud,' Greenspan was referring to Bernie Madoff," says Patrick Byrne, when asked to comment on his relationship to these events. "By 'securitization,' Greenspan was referring to the role played by mortgage-backed securities in the 2008 financial crisis. But when Greenspan said 'settlement,' he was referring to what in 2005-2008 I had been pointing out to anyone who would listen. I had doused myself in gasoline and self-immolated in front of the SEC to warn the country about settlement failures and systemic risk. That day in October 2008 Greenspan told Congress the same thing. Everyone in financial circles knew that I had been proven correct."

It was a fitting denouement to one of the strangest sagas that ever played out on Wall Street. But it is as good a place as any to anchor the story of Patrick Byrne.

According to PBS, Patrick Byrne is now the "kingpin" of the movement that asserts that election integrity is significantly sloppier than is generally understood, that election-rigging now occurs with methods beyond anything that can be discovered through rudimentary audits, and (though he claims he never voted for Trump) that the 2020 election was rigged.

Byrne joined in calling for Americans to rally in DC on January 4–6, 2021. Though he insisted those rallies be peaceful, he has offered to pay the $350,000 of damages to the Capitol Building which get stacked onto the charges of each J6 defendant, making their sentencing more severe. "I look at it this way," says Byrne. "Assume I invited a bunch of friends to a bar and a riot of suspicious origin broke out that evening. As a gesture of goodwill, before we got to the subject of whether my friends or the bouncers started the fight, I might be inclined to pay for the damages. Simply on the principle of, 'They were *my* guests, it got out of hand, I'll cover the broken mirrors and furniture...'"

Byrne closes his thought with a chuckle: "But if there's going to be talk about filing charges, let us look at the security cameras and see who *really* started the riot."

In addition, Byrne has publicly offered to face all nonviolent charges from that day. Those accused can say they did it because they listened to Byrne, and Byrne will agree to stipulate this is true, on the condition he can defend himself in televised proceedings. "I'll face charges for 1,000 of the J6 rally-goers. I won't face charges for anyone who broke a window or touched a cop, but I will for everyone who was peaceful, on the condition that I can defend my actions in a televised trial. Lay it on me, and I will answer for it *all* to a DC jury."

Byrne delivers the idea with no hint of bluster or menace but in a friendly, helpful manner. In a similar tone, he notes that law enforcement from around the country who are receiving training at DHS have gotten word back to Byrne of a phenomenon he calls, "disconcerting."

When trainees ask, "Whom do you fear more, Russia or China?" DHS trainers have been instructed to reply, "We are keeping our eyes on both, but above all we worry about this guy Patrick Byrne and the movement he has going."

According to Byrne, it began happening in the summer of 2022, just months before the 2022 election, "and Law Enforcement who experienced it got in touch to let me know that DHS is telling people I am Domestic Extremist Threat #1," says Byrne with a broad grin.

Over the years, Byrne's trajectory has reminded some of the character Colonel Kurz from *Apocalypse Now*—an early "golden boy" who goes off track through (say some) insanity, genius, or some dark impulse that cannot be unraveled. Now for the first time since his departure from acceptable society, Byrne has sat long enough to give a comprehensive interview touching upon all corners of his life and activities.

Because it is easy to find Byrne's manner and language disorienting, some sections of this interview will not be summarized, but will remain as Q&A transcript, for the reader to digest directly.

CHAPTER 1

THE ODD TALE OF PATRICK BYRNE

A. BYRNE'S BOYHOOD

"My life has had so many tailwinds it is almost comical," answers Byrne when asked about his origins. "It is easy and not inappropriate to see it as a silver spoon. The truth is slightly more interesting: over my first twenty-five years my family lived a Horatio Alger dream, and I saw it unfold." Asked to expand, Byrne answers, "For the 1960s the Byrne family was Tuna-Helper, for the 1970s it was Hamburger-Helper, by the 1980s it was steak and lobster, by the 1990s it was King Airs, and from 2000 onward, private jets."

Only after some prodding does Byrne go into details. According to him, "Both parents are from New Jersey Irish working-class backgrounds. My mother's father was a lineman in Cape May, New Jersey. My father's side was from Patterson tenements that were then Irish and Jewish, by the 1960s were Black and Hispanic, and are now Muslim. In the Depression they moved to Wildwood. Pop went Air Force ROTC to

Rutgers, ticked off a general, served his years in an ice station in northern Greenland, discharged and married Mom. On the G.I. Bill, broke-as-a-joke, they moved to University of Michigan so Pop could get a master's in actuarial Math and land an insurance job, which had been his dream since he was ten, oddly. Michigan and Indiana are where we three kids popped into existence. Our dear middle brother passed away several years ago."

"While I was an infant, we moved to New England. My father bounced among jobs in Massachusetts and Connecticut, which is where I went to grade school, but our family time was all in Vermont and New Hampshire, which began to feel more like home."

Byrne tells a story about his youth. "Since childhood, our folks' message was, 'We will support you through your education, but then you are on your own. Nothing can make us prouder than you focusing on education, but that is that all you are owed.'" And he launches into a story that ultimately reveals his connections to Washington, DC.

B. PATRICK BYRNE GOES TO WASHINGTON

When Byrne was thirteen his father was passed over for a promotion at an insurance firm in Hartford, The Travelers. "When I was older, he let me know that he felt it was because he was Irish Catholic, in the mold of Tip O'Neil: a big, chubby, garrulous Irishman. He also hired Jews and Blacks. How he saw it, the WASPs at HQ liked him because of his ability to work with insurance agents, who were often Jewish or Black because they start small insurance agencies to avoid big-firm discrimination. But the Brass did not want Jews and Blacks at HQ and opposed a Catholic rising too high. "The promotion went instead to a WASP out of Hollywood Central Casting, a man who never made his numbers, who over the next twenty years ran The Travelers into the ground," says Byrne the younger. "I was with my father in his dying days and that setback haunted him, though for decades I told him it was the best thing that ever happened to the Family Byrne."

Why that was the best thing that ever happened to the Byrne family became clear as the story continues. "Pop quit in disgust and took a job at a failing car insurance firm down here in the South, a job for which they could find no one else because it was near bankrupt. An actuary was an odd choice to run a car insurance company, but like I said, they could find no one else. So in 1976 we moved to Maryland. He was at his new job only a week or two before he came home and said that he had a plan to save the firm. It would be...energetic."

Weeks into it, his father received a message that a Nebraska stockbroker wanted to meet and talk about what he was doing. "My dad went to see him and did not come home until dawn. He had never done anything like that. When he came back in the morning he told us, "I've just met the smartest man I've ever met in my life. He is some kind of farmer-investor.""

Byrne continues, "Our family had our order in for our first new car, a $7,000 station wagon. Pops promised it to my mom to assuage her about our sudden move. But that morning he told us we were canceling the new car and buying stock in his new friend. It turned out that new friend was excited about the meeting also, because he went out and bet big on my dad."

Finally, Byrne drops his reveal. "That new job of my dad was at GEICO, which almost disappeared in 1976. And his new Best Friend Forever was Warren Buffett." At the time, GEICO was 1/100th its current size, and Buffett was virtually unknown.

According to Byrne, Buffett bet one-third of his net worth on Byrne's dad, and that became Buffett's first billion. "That $7,000 car, invested instead in Berkshire Hathaway stock in 1976, along with the rest of that decade at GEICO, worked out ridiculously well for the Byrne family."

These years played out as Byrne attended high school at Bethesda's Walt Whitman High, '81 (a National Merit Scholar who went All-State in Football both ways, and county champion wrestler before taking up boxing at a DC gym called "Findley's Gym"). "I was the youngest and smallest of three boys," explains Byrne. "I grew up getting my ass kicked by my two big brothers. So, while they learned to golf and kayak, as soon as I was able, I wanted to learn to wrestle, box, and study whatever martial arts were handy."

During those years, Buffett would occasionally visit and stay with Byrne's family. "Mr. Buffett would call ahead and tell my folks, 'Have Patrick be home next Thursday at 11:00 a.m. for two hours.' In Dorothy Byrne's household there was no such thing as 'skipping school,' but my parents were so enamored of this guy from Nebraska that they would pull me out of school just so I could sit with him for a few hours. Once I got a message from him, 'I'll be in New York City next week, come by such-and-such a hotel and spend Tuesday afternoon with me, 2-4 PM.' One summer, I found myself hitchhiking around the county and he had me stop in Omaha to take me to dinner at Gorat's, which has since become famous in Buffett-World."

Somewhere in those years, Byrne says, he and Buffett started to use the term "Rabbi" to describe Buffett's relationship to Byrne (because it resembled the relationship a young Jewish boy would have with his own Rabbi). "It was absurdly generous of Mr. Buffett, looking back," says Byrne. "I was thirteen, maybe fourteen when it started. I still remember verbatim parables Buffett told me. My life's direction was changed by those afternoons he took for me. As was my father's life. After ten years at GEICO, he moved on and spent the rest of his career repeating what he had done at GEICO, fixing broken insurance companies with Warren Buffett as his partner."

Byrne describes his first foray into entrepreneurship. While a sophomore at Whitman High in Bethesda, he and his brothers ran a Christmas Tree business out of a parking lot off McArthur Boulevard. Byrne can still recite the numbers: "500 trees bought for $8/tree in Maine and trucked down in a Ryder by my oldest brother, that we then sold in Bethesda for $30/tree. That was 500 trees X $22 gross profit =$11,000 in gross profit, minus our expenses."

Byrne and his brothers sold Christmas trees by a trashcan fire for four years, he says. "The first year we were making money on paper, but two days before Christmas 40 percent of our trees were unsold. That is when I first learned about 'overstock'. Two days before Christmas we gave them away to a Korean church in Virginia. But the second and third years, we netted about $8,000 with two weeks' work, and thought we had discovered the wheel. Then the fourth year someone else opened up in the same lot, and we learned why Buffett says, 'Allah loves a monopoly.'"

In 1981 Byrne graduated from Bethesda's Walt Whitman High School. "I had a great experience at Whitman, where a fantastic principle named Dr. Jerome Marcose led a fine institution. I had teachers and coaches with whom I stayed in touch for years out of gratitude for how they touched my life. I had wonderful friends throughout those years, whom I remember fondly. But I could not wait to go back to New England, and the day after I graduated, I moved back to New England.

"Growing up around New England, especially northern New England, meant that by nature we were not flatlanders. The Byrne Family had spent all our non-school time in New Hampshire and Vermont, and over time, those states came to feel most like home. Maybe that is why I have always been conscious of being around city people. You know how to city folk, people from the country seem odd? It works the other way around, too. Frankly, to people from the country, city people seem like *kooks*. What passes for normal behavior in city environments will, if you do it in the country, lead people to think you're an idiot.

So the day after I graduated from Whitman, I drove to a farm in Vermont, which became my favorite period in life."

C. COLLEGE YEARS

Byrne moved to Vermont, and he soon joined his two older brothers at Dartmouth College, in nearby Hanover, New Hampshire. Why did all three boys go to Dartmouth when his father had gone to Rutgers? "Because of that attachment to northern New England, we had always assumed Dartmouth would be the place, when the time came."

At Dartmouth Byrne majored in Philosophy (the Western kind, his favorite course being logic) and Asian Studies. He played football for two years and worked on the farm. "I was a grind," says Byrne, "and decided that while at college I would never enter a party, a fraternity, or a church. I did not want to be in a room where everyone felt pressure to think the same way. I worked on the farm, and two or three days per week I was in class and spent a great deal of time in the library and language lab. Seasons went by where I spent days in the library and evenings studying Chinese."

Giving up his last two years of college football in 1983, Byrne went to China as it opened to foreign students, spending a year at Beijing Teacher's University. Initially he studied Chinese language but went on to history and philosophy. "It started with Laozi, Zhuangzi, Confucius, and a certain Tang Dynasty writer I admired, but I continued through Marxist-Leninist-Maoist thought."

In 1983, seven years after the Cultural Revolution, Patrick Byrne was in Beijing studying Maoism? "Yep," he replies cheerfully, and speaks in Chinese regarding Dialectical Materialism and the Cultural Revolution.

From China Byrne went to Thailand for six months, studied Thai language and kickboxing, returned home to the US to graduate after writing a thesis in each of his Dartmouth majors. One was a translation from Classical Chinese, the other, on Marx. "I was already trying to work out what was wrong," he tells me. "I had these wonderful teachers, both in China and in the US, who were Lefties. I suppose I was trying to make sense out of how that could be, how people so smart in so many ways were so backward in others. But I could not put my finger on it."

In that endeavor he was guided by two philosophy professors visiting Dartmouth when Byrne returned. David Luban, now a Georgetown Law professor, and his wife, Judith Lichtenberg, of Georgetown Philosophy, both distinguished philosophers. "David is known in many sub-disciplines such as Legal Ethics and is a major figure in the Torture Debate," says Byrne. "Judy is a social and moral philosopher." Byrne says that both are highly regarded and associated with the Left.

"We've maintained an intellectual friendship for decades, one that generally transcended our political differences. But now that DHS tells people I am Domestic Extremist Threat #1, things may be a bit chilly,"

Byrne says, sadly. "When they come to understand that I was right about elections, I fear they will never forgive me."

D. CANCER + ACADEMIA

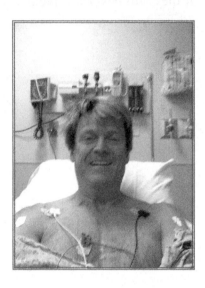

Immediately upon graduating Dartmouth in 1985, Byrne was diagnosed with cancer. It would hit him three times in his twenties, which were largely spent dealing with cancer and convalescing. He declines to discuss the subject, saying only, "I have told that story once publicly, and once was enough."[1]

Byrne limits himself to dropping a few statistics about his health. Of roughly 22,000 nights on Earth, Byrne says, he has spent over 800 in hospitals. He draws his collar aside and reveals a fresh surgical scar near the base of his neck, not even a week old, still bandaged. "Last week I had surgery #115. They removed a tumor. It was benign, *humd'allah*. I've also had my heart stopped about 400 times. So I've ridden that Death Train about 500 times."

Each of the three times Byrne had cancer, he had hospital stays lasting up to six months. When he left the hospital after each of his three

---

1. https://www.pmc.org/blog/ pmc-threshold-moment-by- billy-starr

bouts, as a way of rebuilding himself Byrne flew to California, bought a bicycle, and rode east until to the Atlantic Ocean, increasing his push-ups and pull-ups throughout every day of the journey. The latter two trips were solo, but he completed the first with his oldest brother, John, and their middle brother Mark joined them in Houston to finish the trip. Byrne's parents tracked them down on a Louisiana highway and provided support their last 400 miles: Byrne believes the resulting photo, taking outside Jacksonville, Florida, with just a few miles left to pedal, is the last photo of his nuclear family together as one unit.

During his years in-and-out of hospital in his twenties, Byrne began graduate studies in mathematical logic at Stanford University, in Palo Alto, California. "Stanford Philosophy was tremendous to me, and those studies brought me close to a religious experience," says Byrne. "One hears about a botanist studying a flower and seeing God in the petals of a rose. For me, it was that period of studying logic. One night I left Greene Library at midnight to ride home in the dark, and as I bicycled, I had what I suppose was a religious experience. For some it is the Bible, for some it is a rose, for me it was Computation Theory."

At Stanford Byrne first encountered what he calls "Early Woke," seeing it as "Maoism with American characteristics," says Byrne. He describes the worldview of Marxists:

"'The world is divided into knaves and fools, and we need to stop the knaves from oppressing the fools.' That presupposes a third class of individuals, 'experts' who will make decisions for BOTH fools and knaves in order to prevent that oppression. Unfortunately, history has shown that people drawn to that position of 'expert' are almost invariably authoritarians with a desire to rule others, which they mask in the language of compassion."

Byrne continues, "Let's go from Marxism to Maoism. Mao came to power in 1949, but by the 1960s he was being put out to pasture, having made mistakes such as, The Great Leap Forward. So he called for a 'Cultural Revolution,'" Byrne explains. "In the ideology of the Cultural Revolution, there were five bad kinds of people: landlords, capitalists, rich peasants, right-wingers, and anti-revolutionaries. Adults in these bad categories were humiliated, trotted around with dunce caps, tortured, rusticated, even killed. Worse yet, their children inherited their 'Bad.' The only way out of it for the children was to adopt a new identity: 'Red.'"

"Map that onto what is occurring here: 'Bad' identities are White, male, Christian, Cis. 'Good' identities are 'intersectional' and an alternate identity with which all youth can redeem themselves is 'Woke' or eighty-seven flavors of 'Queer.'"

Byrne concludes, "This is Maoist 'Movement Warfare' with American characteristics, *mutatis mutandis*."

Byrne won a Marshall Fellowship and went to Cambridge University in England for two years, switching from logic to moral and political philosophy, and studying with legends of philosophy and economics. There he also encountered Full Woke "anti-intellectual, uninformed… about what current US university life has become many places." Still convalescing and in-and-out of hospitals, Byrne returned to Stanford and discovered that in just a few years it had started reorienting on a Woke agenda. He found himself reacting against this academic environment. "I found myself shifting more towards political philosophy, trying to understand how people who were good, decent, and smart in so many ways could be willing to jettison the values and principles underlying Constitutional republicanism for stale, uninformed Marxist bromides."

At Stanford Byrne had studied the origin of Western principles such as tolerance, free speech, and rights of the accused, but found those principles unraveling at a great American university. "I had always looked at World War II differently than teachers wanted us. In high school they wanted to tell us that the great lesson of WWII was, 'Don't be nationalistic.' That seemed incorrect. The great lesson from World War II was, 'When authoritarians challenge the values of political liberalism, defend them immediately. Don't surrender an inch.'"

Yet in the early 1990s Byrne saw these values abandoned in university "culture wars." Now he says a glorious 2,500-year-old intellectual tradition is at risk of being lost to what he calls "a horde of intellectuals who have had no deep commitment to those principles and lack knowledge of history and economics."

E. ENTREPRENEURSHIP

During and after completing his PhD, Byrne worked in a variety of entrepreneurial endeavors. He was involved with liquidating real estate out of the S&L crisis, worked on Wall Street for a year, and led a land deal involving the construction of a casino in Colorado. He then led a variety of investment groups making small investments in business deals in northern New England and around the county.

"A Jiffy Lube in Florida needed to be bought out from TWA pilot getting a divorce. We'd buy it, tweak it a bit, refinance and get the capital into real estate in Manchester, New Hampshire. Then sell that project to get the capital into a printing company in Providence, Rhode Island. Then a Fixed-Base-Operator at an airport in New Jersey. On and on."

Eventually Byrne ended up the majority owner/ CEO of a twenty-person machine-shop telemarketing industrial parts from Lebanon, New Hampshire, for three years. He led a small team of investors, many from high school and college, in acquiring the firm for $6 million.

"We hired some engineers and made a huge innovation in Computer Numerically Controlled Automation ("CNC Automation") by building the first CNC controllers not using specially-burned EPROM ("Electronically Programmed Read-Only Memory") chips and similar expensive components, but from off-the-shelf parts. In that way we harnessed the pricing power of the consumer electronics revolution and reduced the cost of making a CNC-controller by about 80 percent. We were the first in the world to do this, and it so threatened the CNC industry that we sold four years later for $24 million. Looking back, it was probably far too cheap. But it gave me the capital I needed to get going."

That is when Buffett called asked Byrne to come plug a gap for him for three months...that turned into two magical years. Byrne describes working for the man who had been his "Rabbi" since he was a teenager, but it is clear he feels uncomfortable revealing details about their friendship. "I can talk about things he taught me," says Byrne. "But I tend to avoid going into detail about our relationship. That was our deal from the start."

By 1999 Byrne's unusual background in both entrepreneurship and academia was leading to offers to teach at business schools and even to run leadership institutes then popping up in US universities. Byrne was considering settling down to the life of a professor but started one last project: Overstock.com.

With no venture capital or institutional backing, Byrne launched Overstock. He ran Overstock.com on the old-fashioned principles that Buffett had taught him rather than the new economics of the dot-com bubble. Byrne pioneered innovations in digital marketing (such as introducing Wall Street arbitrage techniques into the nascent world of online advertising) and supply-chains (such as "agile networked supply chains" and "B2C drop-shipping") that became part of the fabric of e-commerce. In just a few years Byrne turned Overstock profitable on tens of millions of dollars in capital compared to the hundreds of millions (or billions used by competitors such as Amazon).

Over twenty years, Byrne's "one last project" emerged as a $2 billion giant, while Byrne earned accolades as *National Entrepreneur of the Year* (2011) and Overstock as one of the *100 Most Trusted Businesses in America (2014)* out of 8,000 public firms.

F. THE HISTORIC WALL STREET SCUFFLE

It was during those years that Byrne got into his notorious fight with Wall Street. He says that as a public company CEO starting in 2002, he was meeting with various Wall Street players. Eventually, he says, he began to be taken to dinner and have muttered to him offers that began, *Hey kid, we could make a lotta money together... if you're willing to play ball.*

In Byrne's telling, he responded by doing what he thought any citizen would do: he reverse-engineered their schemes then went to the authorities to explain what was going on.

"Their indolence was overwhelming," Byrne adds.

By 2005 Byrne was in a battle over aspects of the Wall Street financial plumbing (the "settlement system") that, he claimed, allowed hedge funds to manipulate markets and destabilize the system. He came to claim that the SEC was not truly policing Wall Street but inappropriately close to it and introduced into popular usage the economists' term "regulatory capture." In Byrne's telling, the SEC pursued small fry but was afraid to police the worst players" on Wall Street either because they had "too much juice" (as in 2008 an SEC official was caught saying about Morgan Stanley's CEO[2]), or because they were thinking of their future employment, and understood lucrative offers await only those who "regulate" lightly.

"Milton Friedman famously said, 'There is no such thing as a free lunch.' As hedge funds and the finance industry use such schemes to earn billions or trillions, those dollars are coming from somewhere. They are drained from the retirement accounts of Americans," says Byrne. "If one were walking down an alley and saw an old lady being mugged, one would get up in someone's grill about it. So I went public about my beliefs. Unfortunately, I still thought the world worked like something out of *The Pelican Brief.* You know: Julia Roberts figures out the evil corporation's scheme, writes up her term paper, the DOJ, and the *Washington Post* swoop in to investigate..."

Byrne guffaws at the depths of his early innocence. "No, what really happens is that all that corruption turns out to feed a lot of mouths, seen and unseen, and when challenged those forces emerge to distort, suppress, and bury truth. Like what we are living through now."

In this battle, Byrne began to be helped by a swarm of people he met

---

2. See "THE FIRING OF AN SEC ATTORNEY AND THE INVESTIGATION OF PEQUOT CAPITAL MANAGEMENT" PREPARED BY THE MINORITY STAFF OF THE COMMITTEE ON FINANCE (Chairman CHARLES E. GRASSLEY) AND THE COMMITTEE ON THE JUDICIARY UNITED STATES SENATE (ARLEN SPECTER, Ranking Member) loaded at https://www.deepcapture.com/wp-content/uploads/36960.pdf

on Internet message boards, an army of activists cooperating to clean up Wall Street. It included researchers and investigators, stockbrokers, economists, lawyers, and engineers who became an extended irregular force in support of the mission. "The *pajamahadeen*," says Byrne. "That is what I called them. It's like being a *mujahedeen*, but you get to do it from your mommy's basement in your pajamas," he jokes.

Byrne's pursuit of "Wall Street mischief" split into two tracks, he explains.

On the one track, he and his *pajamahadeen* were trying to figure out the various sources and ramifications of what Byrne calls, "slop in Wall Street's settlement system." It was that slop to which in October 2008 Greenspan would join Byrne in pointing as one of the primary causes of the 2008 Financial Crisis.

Yet to Byrne, the second and more important track became, "'How does Washington, DC, react to the evidence we are surfacing?' That became an even more important mystery to unravel. I had Harvard PhD economists, I had Wall Street insiders, I had folks from the underbelly of it all, and I had data. I knew that these settlement issues would lead to crisis, and in the meantime, mom-and-pop investors were being ripped off, firms were destroyed, capital was misallocated. I went to see all the people one would first think of seeing: the financial press, the SEC, FINRA, NASD, the House Financial Services Committee, the Senate Banking Committee... We discovered no matter what data or witnesses I brought, they were all frozen."

Glumly, Byrne explains that Congressional staffers started coming clean: "Every time you are here, Byrne, you should know that Goldman and Morgan are in ten times, and you know, they are large supports of the Senator ..."

Byrne tells about the day in 2006 that his assistant ran into his office, panicked: "The Department of Justice is on the phone!"

Byrne told her to put it through, and when he did, Caller ID confirmed it was the DOJ. When Byrne answered, a male voice identified himself as Ken Breen, Assistant United States Attorney. Byrne says he jumped to his feet and stood at attention, cradling the phone to his ear, stammering, "Y-y-es, Sir! How can I help you?" He adds now, chuckling, "It was completely spontaneous and natural. I just held the DOJ in that high regard."

Breen started: "First, I want you to know that it is legal for me to be calling you. I gave my notice to the DOJ several weeks ago, and today is my last day at the Department of Justice. I've packed my office possessions into a banker's box, and in five minutes I am walking out the door to start a new job. But I wanted my last act at the DOJ to be calling you, and you to know there is nothing illegal about me doing so."

Byrne says he gulped. "Yes, Sir. I understand."

Breen continued, "I want you to know that at the DOJ there are thirty or forty people following everything you are doing... and cheering you on. You are doing the right thing. We were looking at ..." then shared a bit of their knowledge of how the hedge fund mischief had evolved. He closed saying they thought I was going down a blind alley regarding one thing I was talking about publicly, but had I looked into this *other* area and considered such-and-such...? Then he started wrapping up his call."

Byrne says he was flabbergasted, and finally responded, "Sir, thank you and please thank your colleagues. But I have to ask one thing: Why are *you* telling *me* this? You are a United States Attorney. Can't you folks do something about this...?"

"Breen cut me off," says Byrne, "saying words will ring in my ear to my dying day: 'Oh Patrick, you have no idea how politicized the environment is within which prosecution decisions are made.'" Then Breen hung up.

Byrne tells a story about the English Philosopher Bertrand Russell who in the early 1920s was in India lecturing on the structure of the cosmos per Einstein's new theories. In the midst of one of his university lectures, goes the story, a Hindu professor stood up and said, "I'm sorry Professor Russell, you are incorrect. The universe rides on the back of a turtle."

Russell replied, "Oh really? Then what does the turtle ride on?"

"The back of another turtle," said the Hindu.

"OK, then what's *that* turtle ride on?" answered Bertrand Russell.

The Hindu replied, "I'm sorry Professor Russell, but it's turtles all the way down!"

Byrne laughs at the story, but then explains, "From 2005 forward we had everything one needed to understand what was going to happen in 2008, what Greenspan would tell Congress in October 2008 was at the core of the financial crisis: settlement. The data, the economists, the experts, the insiders. For three years we took it all to the financial press, the SEC, FINRA, NASD, House Financial, and Senate banking... and we found that it was just turtles all the way down."

Byrne's accusations of "regulatory capture" at the SEC were initially dismissed as "conspiracy theory." CNBC and the financial press tarred-and-feathered Byrne for two years.

In January 2007, Byrne and his cousin (a well-known Wall Street figure) were invited to tea by Richard Chilton, whom Byrne calls "a greybeard" of the industry. Chilton opened the meeting saying calmly, "Patrick, I want you to know you have become the most hated man I've ever known in my entire life. You used to be something of a Golden Boy around here on Wall Street, but now you could kill people and not be hated like you are hated here now."

Byrne says he replied without hesitation, "Sir, I stand by everything I've done."

Now Byrne adds with a conspiratorial whisper, "Ain't that high fucking praise? Please carve on my tombstone, 'Here lies The Most Hated Man on Wall Street 2007!" He chuckles. "And now you can add, 'and Joe Biden's DHS Domestic Extremist Threat #1!'"

By 2007 there were some people who began wondering if Byrne's criticisms of Wall Street were correct. News stories appeared raising that possibility, such as a Bloomberg special entitled, *Phantom Shares*, which was nominated for an Emmy Award.

Then the crisis of 2008 exploded. Alan Greenspan was in Congress explaining that the crisis was found not just in fraud (Madoff) and securitization (mortgage-backed securities), but in precisely that "settlement system" Byrne had been warning about for three years. At the same time, the unhealthy relationship between the SEC and Wall Street was exposed to the general public until it went from a conspiracy theory to the stuff of late-night comedy.

As the 2008 crisis unfolded along precisely the lines Byrne had been predicting for three years, the press began writing things such as, "These days, when people talk of Byrne, the word 'vindication' comes up a lot..." And the *Wall Street Journal* named Byrne among the five who had seen it coming.

THE WALL STREET JOURNAL.

English Edition ▾ | Print Edition | Video | Audio | Latest Headlines | More ▾

World   Business   U.S.   Politics   Economy   Tech   Finance   Opinion   Arts & Culture   Lifestyle   Real Estate   Pe

2008 Lookback: Best Calls of the Year

By David Gaffen
Dec. 23, 2008 3:33 pm ET

↪ Share   A A Resize

In a year when major stock indexes, real estate, hedge funds, oil, grains, emerging markets, dollar/yen, long/short hedging strategies (thanks to the short-selling ban), high-yield bonds, bank loans, diversification, and the Super Bowl Indicator failed investors, there were precious few "calls" that worked out

---

Naked shorting's early critic starts to see some vindication

Submitted by cpowell on Sun, 2008-08-03 23:56 Section: Daily Dispatches

Byrne's Battle Helps Bring Curbs on Naked Short-Selling Practices

By Steven Oberbeck
The Salt Lake Tribune
Saturday, August 2, 2008

http://www.sltrib.com/ci_10079510

Over the past several years, Patrick Byrne's campaign to clean up Wall Street and end a practice that has destroyed companies and cost unwary investors billions of dollars generated plenty of publicity for him, mostly the wrong kind.

Critics labeled him nuts, a conspiracy theorist, a complete wack job.

Byrne, the chief executive of the Utah-based discount online retailer Overstock.com, even found himself tagged a member of the "tin-foil hat" brigade, a reference to the flying saucer fanatics of the 1950s who adorned their heads with aluminium to ward off, or enhance, thoughts from aliens in outer space.

These days, when people talk of Byrne, the word "vindication" comes up a lot.

"You can always tell who the pioneers are -- they're the ones with all the arrows sticking out of their backs," said James Angel, a finance professor at Georgetown University. "You really can't understate what Byrne has accomplished."

Three years ago Byrne, believing Overstock.com's shares were under pressure from an illegal trading tactic known as "naked short-selling," launched a campaign to end the practice. He termed it his own personal "jihad," or holy war.

Short-selling is a legal practice in which brokerages allow investors to borrow and then sell a company's stock on the hope its price will drop. If that happens, investors then can buy back the stock at a lower price, pocket the profit and return the shares to the brokerages.

Naked short-selling takes place when investors sell stock without first borrowing it. In market parlance, the seller is "naked" those shares. The usual outcome that it creates an artificially high volume of shares for sale, which can drive down a company's stock price.

In a naked short sale, the transaction is never truly completed because the short-seller doesn't really possess the stock that was sold. That means the seller cannot deliver the shares to buyers, which in market jargon is called a "failure to deliver."

... Big Victory

Byrne's biggest victory in his jihad came July 15 when the U.S. Securities and Exchange Commission issued an emergency order that prohibited naked short-selling in the shares of Fannie Mae, Freddie Mac and 17 large investment banks.

The fear was that aggressive short-selling could exacerbate the plunge in those company's share prices. The SEC goal was to stem the downward pressure on the shares by requiring short-sellers to actually borrow shares before selling them.

"Even though they [the SEC] would never admit it, Patrick Byrne helped instruct them in the danger. When the time came, they understood the threat," said Peter Chepucavage, a former attorney in the SEC's Division of Market Regulation now with the Plexus Consulting Group in Washington, D.C.

Byrne said he supports the SEC's emergency rule, which on Thursday was extended through mid-August. "What I don't understand is why the SEC is only addressing Fannie Mae, Freddie Mac and the large investment banks. Why should those companies be the only ones protected?"

G. BYRNE'S POLITICS

Byrne's political commitments run to what he calls "libertarian republican," with an emphasis, he says, on "small 'l' libertarian and small 'r' republican." The formulation comes from Milton Friedman.

Weeks before he died, Friedman called Byrne, telling him that he and Rose knew the end was near and wanted to make a last change to the will. They had decided to ask Byrne to take over leadership of the Milton & Rose Friedman Foundation for ten years after Friedman's death, before stepping away and changing the name.

Byrne says he was startled at the request but after a moment, agreed, adding, "Sir, this surprises me. I know that on Wall Street I have gotten into it with a bunch of your admirers. I don't have any choice about doing what I am doing, but I know that I've been acting like something of an Irish hothead…."

Friedman thought about his answer for three seconds, "which was two seconds longer than Milton ever needed to think about an answer to anything," according to Byrne.

Finally, Friedman replied, "You know something Pat? Maybe what our side has been missing has been an Irish hothead."

Byrne says that to him, it was as though Isaac Newton had called and said, "Would you carry on in my name for ten years after my death?"

Byrne proudly shows us a page from the National Education Association website in 2008, where the massive union listed its well-known opponents: Wal-Mart and Starbucks were #2 and #3. There on the NEA website, they named the union's Public Enemy #1: Patrick Byrne.

With a grin Byrne says, "So in 2007 I was 'The Most Hated Man on Wall Street,' in 2008 I became the 'NEA's Public Enemy #1,' and in 2022 I became Joe Biden's 'DHS Domestic Extremist #1.' My cup runneth over."

For ten years Byrne led the Milton & Rose Friedman Foundation. After a decade he stepped down and changed the name to "The Foundation for Educational Choice." Located in Indianapolis, Indiana, it remains the intellectual center of gravity of the national movement for educational choice, according to Byrne.

What are Byrne's political ambitions? Without hesitation Byrne replies, "Zero." Minutes later, Byrne is asked again, "Really: What are your political ambitions?"

"Zero. Sub-zero. Zero-degree-Kelvin-zero."

Byrne believes what the country is experiencing is due to capture. "It is as Federalist #10 predicted," says Byrne. "In designing the Constitution, Madison wrote, they looked at previous attempts at Democracy, ancient and modern, looked at what made those experiments fail, and tried to design a better system. But they knew that there was a problem they had not figured out how to solve, and it was the one that took down republics more than any other problem: the problem of special interests and the corruption they bring. A short way of saying, 'special interests and the corruption they bring' is to say, 'capture.'"

Byrne looks pensive. "We have a lot of different problems, in one sense, but the common denominator of them is that of our institutions are failing because of capture, both at the regulatory level, and at deeper levels."

H. "BITCOIN MESSIAH"

Byrne says that it is this frustration with the corruption of institutions that turned him so strongly towards Bitcoin and, more importantly (he says), towards its underlying technology, Blockchain.

In 2013, the largest firm in the world that was taking Bitcoin was a diner in Australia with $800,000/year in revenue. "In dark corners of the internet, Bitcoin-devotees discussed when there might be a million-dollar/year business that would start accepting Bitcoin, then how many years before a $10 million business, how many years before a $100 million business...." says Byrne.

That is when Overstock.com, a $1.5 billion firm, got instructions from Byrne to build the systems that would accept Bitcoin. "The day Overstock began accepting Bitcoin it made news globally," says Byrne. Old-timers in the Bitcoin space often spoke of that decision letting humanity save five–six years in its adoption of Bitcoin, and by extension, crypto-technology.

For Byrne, however, "the real attraction of Bitcoin was not Bitcoin, it was the technology that powers Bitcoin, called "blockchain." The problem described in Federalist #10 by Madison, that institutions get captured and corrupted, had nagged at Byrne for decades. "What I saw in blockchain technology was that it was based on cryptography, which is to say, that area of mathematics called 'Computation Theory' that I had studied at Stanford and about which I had had a religious experience. I saw that one could recreate within blockchain the most important institutions holding society together, and finally have institutions that could not be corrupted. We have seen that oligarchs can corrupt the SEC and DOJ, the regulators and the Congress, the press and academia... but not even oligarchs can corrupt the laws of mathematics," reasons Byrne.

"I picked out the processes that I thought were the most fundamental processes of civilization that would have to be turned into blockchain applications. I started calling that set of processes, "The Blockchain Tech-Stack of Civilization":

1. Land-titling – Because when law has a place to bite, Rule of Law can begin;

2. Money – Because humans communicate about value and scarcity through prices;

3. Capital markets – So that humans can marry financial capital to human capital;

4. Supply chains – So that humans can engage in complex voluntary exchange;

5. Voting – Because voting reveals what it is to which the governed in fact consent.

"Importantly, the whole thing had to be based on an Identity solution that respected the principle of 'Self-Sovereign Identity' lest the whole thing turn into a totalitarian nightmare."

Byrne traveled the world looking for entrepreneurs who had already found these niches and were working in them. Where there were companies that already existed, Byrne met the entrepreneurs and provided angel investment or first round Venture Capital investment. Where no such firm yet existed, "I would find some young entrepreneurs who wanted to get into blockchain and give them the idea, wrote up a term paper for them to follow, and slid a million dollars into it."

Those blockchain firms Byrne created and funded now lead the world in their respective areas. "Medici Land Titling" has numerous contracts across Africa and the US and is recognized as the leading technology in the world for land-titling on the incorruptible blockchain.

For money, Byrne launched the world's first CBDC (Central Bank Digital Currency), a project called "Bitt.com" in Barbados and the Eastern Caribbean Union. He started tZero, a blockchain version of Wall Street which made impossible those settlement failures and other forms of malfeasance against which Byrne had railed in 2005-2008: tZero recently received a $250 million investment from the New York Stock Exchange, which claims they will be taking tZero public soon at a $20 billion valuation. His investment in supply chains, called "GrainChain," is being adopted by farmers ahead of any other.

Only the blockchain voting firm is one about which Byrne now expresses ambivalence. "In a perfect world we *would* use blockchain to vote. But with what I have learned since then, I know the systems are all so corrupt we must start again with pencil-and-paper and move forward from there."

Byrne has another regret about his involvement in blockchain. "Seven years ago, I was invited to the US Treasury to give a talk about my Blockchain Tech-Stack for Humanity. When I got to the part explaining Central Bank Digital Currencies, I emphasized how we had to get this built and out there on an experimental basis in the USA. When they asked me why, I told them that I had been visiting with the equivalent players in China and saw what they were doing. They were building an authoritarian version of what I had designed, one that did not respect Self-Sovereign Identity."

A woman from Treasury in the audience asked me what I meant, and I told her, "The Chinese version allows them to say, 'Madam *your* money counts, and Mister *your* money counts, but this other woman over there? Madam, you tweeted something nice about the Dalai Lama so *your* money doesn't count anymore."

"I will never forget how, instead of chuckling, she looked sharply at a couple of colleagues at the table, poker-faced. I realized that I had either just given someone a bad idea, or I had stumbled over a bad idea they had already grasped. From all indications, the CBDC that they plan on rolling out in the USA is architected like the Chinese version, which will allow them to implement authoritarianism."

I. BYRNE'S METHODS BECOME... *UNSOUND*

So in 2019, there was Byrne, CEO of a $2 billion e-commerce company he built, "National Entrepreneur of the Year" per Ernst & Young, leader of one of "The 100 Most Trusted Companies in America" per Forbes, heralded by *Wired Magazine* as, "The Messiah of Bitcoin" for his early involvement in the field, and recipient of countless awards regarding his visionary leadership and entrepreneurship. Life was good.

But just as with the character of Colonel Kurz, Byrne's methods "became unsound."

It was August 2019 when everything changed. Byrne says, "I was watching my country burn, and I knew the truth about a lot of things in which I had been involved. As things boiled over, I went to see my Rabbi, and in twenty minutes I explained to him what was really going on. I had never seen him angry in my life, but he was angry that day. He paced for twenty seconds then said, *Patrick, your country is burning. The correct analysis is: The truth has to come out. Given that the truth has to come out, the sooner it comes out the better.* He said that it could not be another Grassy Knoll for fifty years, and told me that I had an obligation to go public, regardless of the repercussions for myself."

Weeks later, Byrne resigned from Overstock and went on Fox News with Martha McCallum. He said he had a relationship with the US Government, he had been present for the origins of the Russian Collusion Delusion, and that the entire matter was a hoax. It had all been engineered, Byrne said, and claimed he had helped engineer it. He referred to his involvement in a corruption investigation of a federal official.

Then Byrne flew to Indonesia.

CHAPTER 2:

A CONVERSATION WITH PATRICK BYRNE

We are sitting with Patrick Byrne now. The Durham report has just come out. Byrne says that he knows more about the subject than any man in America. To prove it, he plays a short video of a retired US Attorney Brett Tolman from August 2019, explaining on Fox:[3]

"I know Patrick Byrne. I've known him for years. I spent 45 minutes on the phone with him today talking about it. When he indicates he has previously worked with the FBI and provided information, he's telling the truth. Back in 2005 and 2006, I was chief counsel for the Senate Judiciary Committee, and he brought to us inside information about manipulation that was going on and Wall Street. It turned out that it was accurate, and it was investigated, and it became part of a much larger investigation. So, my experience with him is very fascinating, because while he's eccentric, he has been accurate historically with me and with others."

After playing that video, Byrne shows us a photo of Maria Butina, taken as they strolled through DC.

3. https://rumble.com/v2u1zek-us-attorney-acknowledges-patrick-byrne-on-bonginod

"Connect those two dots, what US Attorney Brett Tolman said in that video and what this photo shows, and you arrive at an insight: I am the most qualified man in America to tell you the truth about the Russia Investigation," says Byrne. "I'll save the DOJ a lot of trouble and stipulate now: If I am lying about this to the public, I am committing sedition. There, that should make it easy to convict me. DOJ won't. Because what I am going to tell you is true."

Byrne continues, "The Durham Report exposes 50 percent of the truth, how politicized was intelligence, how RussiaGate was a hoax, and so on," says Byrne. "But it is also a cover-up of world-historic proportions. It is Volume II of the story, and they have hidden Volume I."

Byrne adds that he might have held his tongue had he confidence that the corruption had been remedied. But he says he sees nothing of the sort, and that this means he must come forward with the rest of the story. In a series of events (the "ReAwaken America Tour") around the country starring General Mike Flynn, Byrne has dropped pieces of the story, a bewildering kaleidoscope of clues that sound like Robert Ludlum meets Thomas Pynchon.

Now for the first time, Byrne's story is being told in print.

Question: What is or was your connection to the United States Government?

I am not a spy, I have never worked for the CIA. But it has been one of the honors of my life that from time to time, on rare occasion, there have been other parts of the government who knew they could call on me to make a small contribution, generally a rather academic contribution, to some effort of theirs, often having to do with peace.

How did this start? Can you give any examples?

In 1983 I was a student in Beijing. I had a French girlfriend, another foreign student. By day I spoke Chinese, by night, French. One evening she and I were walking through a public place, and a small Asian man overheard us and came bounding up to us speaking French. It turned out he was from Laos and was a general who had run a *coup* in his country years earlier, then been deposed. He was living in a state guesthouse in Beijing. Over a few dinners he and I became friends. Eventually he told me he had written a letter that he wanted me to deliver to the US. I thought about it for a couple days, decided it seemed harmless enough, and did it.

My life for the next five years was intense. I stayed on eighteen months in Asia, returned to the US, wrote two college theses, graduated, collapsed with cancer, spent a few years hospitalized, and began graduate studies at Stanford. I was focused on mathematical logic, but enjoying excursions into other areas, including development economics.

One day at Stanford I got a message: Chairman of the Joint Chiefs General Vessey knew about the letter I had delivered five years earlier and wanted to meet me. I went to northern Minnesota, and we spent a day together.

General Jack Vessey was Reagan's two-term Chairman of the Joint Chiefs. As Vessey was retiring, Reagan asked that, as his last service to the USA, he re-establish peaceful relations with Vietnam. Vessey made some trips to Vietnam. His counterpart Foreign Minister Nguyen Co Thach eventually told him, "If you Americans are serious, please do something humanitarian for us as a sign."

Vessey spent a day getting to know me, quizzing me, actually. Then he asked me to go to Vietnam, where we had no diplomatic relations, but to whom I would be identified as having been sent by General Vessey. I would be hosted by the Vietnamese government. I was to come back with a report for the General as to how $250,000–$300,000 could be spent doing the most humanitarian good for Vietnam.

Why me? I was not an Old Asian Hand, but I was indeed a *Young* Asian Hand. I spoke Chinese, French, and even adequate Thai back then. I had good knowledge of Vietnam from the French conquest up through the Indochinese wars. I also was at Stanford studying Development Economics and had grown up an entrepreneur in an entrepreneurial household.

I went to Hanoi and was hosted by the Foreign Ministry of Vietnam for two extraordinary weeks. I returned and wrote what was in essence a term paper with a dozen good ideas, all priced out with crude attempts at measuring human suffering reduction per dollar. For example, the Swedes had built a small plant that made artificial limbs, but years earlier it had run out of raw material. I calculated how many limbs could be produced from $100 of polyurethane and thus how many lives restored.

I found a dozen opportunities like that. I wrote them up in a term paper, estimating lives improved for every $100 in cost, and submitted it to General Vessey. My understanding is that the US then did all of my projects other than one (installing a large sound system throughout a Blind Person's Nail Factory in Haiphong: I returned in 1989 and did it myself).

It was simple, back-of-the-napkin type stuff. I was perplexed as to how my work could possibly be of service to the United States Government. With the benefit of decades of hindsight, of course, I understand better. To take a conventional approach to a nation with whom the USA had been at war and with which it had no diplomatic relations and sending to it a fact-finding mission to conduct the same analysis.... [Byrne laughs] Now I know enough to understand why General Vessey did what he did. A conventional approach would have included months of oversight, government lawyers signing off on things, and cost millions of dollars. Instead, he found a grad student with some relevant knowledge whom he could send over to spend a couple weeks and come back with his term paper in hand, all inside of a month and for about $5,000 in expense.

Importantly, in 1988 I was identified to the Vietnamese government as doing this favor for the United States Government. As Vietnam was a Soviet client state at the time, one must assume that the Soviets, and hence the Soviet KGB, learned this about me as well. That means that in 1988, the Soviet KGB learned I was doing a humanitarian favor for the USG. Thus, in case you are wondering, I have never had anything to do with our Intelligence Community. When one is identified to the Soviet KGB in 1988 as doing something for Uncle Sam, it makes it impossible to work for the CIA. I had never expected to, but since that is the first-place people's minds might go, I thought it best to clear it up.

Anyway, I don't claim any great credit; I did nothing but make the tiny contribution I described. But it greased the next step, and the next... anyway, it took more years of back and forth between Foreign Minister Nguyen Co Thach and General Vessey, but by 1994 peaceful relations were restored.

General Vessey passed away eight years ago but he had a protégé, General William Nash, who might be able to confirm that story.

So what can you tell us about what came next?

I'm not excited about going into it much. It has been the honor of my life that on a *rare* occasion, I've had opportunity to field a request from some part of the US government, so it feels dishonorable speaking of it publicly, and I assumed word of it would never reach the world until after my death, if ever. But these are odd times, and I have no choice.

One thing I should make clear is that my contribution has primarily been academic: they invite me to come to a government facility and share my thoughts on a subject, usually one I have been writing and speaking about publicly. I get a month's notice, I show up and deliver a PowerPoint with my thoughts, then I am escorted out and that is the last I hear of it.

Here is a good example of the kind of talk it has been my occasional honor to present in government circles. Some years ago, I spoke on "Economic Warfare as an Instrument of Transnational Organized Crime" to the Institute for World Politics in Washington, DC.[4] That talk is based on a talk I gave on other occasions in government settings.

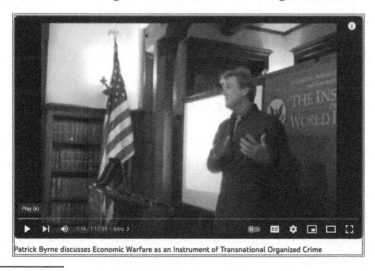

Patrick Byrne discusses Economic Warfare as an Instrument of Transnational Organized Crime

---

4. https://www.youtube.com/watch?v=6FiAHVxCrbQ

So, if you want to know what I mean by saying that the core of my relationship has been academic, and the government invites me to give PowerPoints, watch that link and you will get a good idea. Evidently my name is in some database as a "Designated Expert," though an expert in *what*, no one has ever really explained.

But it also means that on rare, rare occasion, I might get contacted and be asked to do something like what I just described about Vietnam in 1988. Generally, it has to do with an opportunity for peace.

A couple of decades ago, I asked an NSC official making a request of me, "Why do you folks ask me to do these things? Are you that hard up?"

He said, "Patrick, sometimes in this world, before certain kinds of people talk, other kinds of people need to talk. You're… that *other* kind of person."

Because it has been such an honor, talking about it feels disloyal. I am sorry to reveal what I have told you. But I do not have any alternative to share what I am going to share.

Three additional points will become relevant. One concerns security clearances, one concerns Iran, one concerns Venezuela.

First, because of this side-gig of mine, I head a security clearance for me for many years so I could receive briefings. That becomes relevant when I explain the Russian Collusion Delusion.

The second is that around twenty years ago, whenever I was in Asia there seemed to be Iranians making a point to bump me, invite me to come to Iran. In 2006 I was directed (if I was willing) to accept one of these invitations. I got a very open-ended tasking: *accept the next invitation you get, Byrne, go to Iran, socialize, and see where you end up.*

I went to Beirut and gave a talk at a university there regarding corruption and development. Some Iranians in the audience befriended me afterwards and invited me to Tehran. I went, schmoozed, and swanked and *schlemiel*-ed around for a week, gave a talk on John Rawls, and came back Best Friends Forever with General Qassim Suleimani, and the Quds Forces were my boys.

For a decade I have heard that the Iranians tell people there would have been war between Iran and the USA in 2006 were it not for events set in motion by my visit. I do not know why, however, because after I came back other people took over.

In addition, and again, I am only sharing this because it is relevant later: when I left Overstock in 2019, I went SCUBA diving in Indonesia. Suleimani sent word that a war was coming and Iran wanted to ask the USG to have me act as interlocutor, as the American they trusted. I let him know I was hesitant, as I was half on-the-run from the USA, but I sent word.

This was autumn 2019 and given everything else going on, the answer I got from USG was what I can only describe as confused and indecisive. In addition, it was getting difficult for me not only to surf, but even to walk, due to what would prove a tumor on my spinal cord. So I declined General Suleimani's request.

Two months later the USA assassinated Qassim Suleimani.

I do regret that I did not give that one more of the old college try. As a World War II veteran General Vessey used to teach me, "Any world where Russia, China, and the US get along is better than any world in which we three do not get along."

I know from personal experience the war going on today is the most avoidable war of our lifetime. It was so avoidable, it makes me suspicious it was manufactured, quite possibly out of domestic political considerations.

I wish I had sucked it up and made that trip.

The third story I will mention (and again, I tell these three prefatory stories only because they become relevant later) is that in 2018 I was in Venezuela. There was something upon which Venezuela and the USG could have cooperated to the benefit of both, and I was trying to find out if it was possible. The enmity proved such that it turned out to be impossible. But I had an interesting time in Venezuela.

I only mention this one because more recently, during Election 2020, I made claims regarding the computer science capabilities of Venezuelan government. From that herd of independent minds that is modern American journalism the response was, *Byrne, what the hell do you think you know about the Venezuelan government's computer science capabilities?*

This is from the official Instagram account of the Venezuelan Government, March 6, 2018. That is I, standing in a government computer science center in Caracas, Venezuela.

Let that stand for my response to 90 percent of the criticism I receive. Pseudo-intellectual journalists run their mouths without any idea what they are talking about and no awareness of how tedious they are. I think back to university and remember that the students wanting to go into journalism were invariably the second-dumbest students in any course I ever took or taught (the *dumbest* students being football players, which I can say because I was one).

OK then. Fast forward to 2015. How did you get tangled up in current events?

Have you seen the clip of Maria Butina asking candidate Donald Trump a question at a conference in Las Vegas in July 2015?

Yes.

That was 2015 FreedomFest, a libertarian event that occurs in Las Vegas each summer.

Here is that conference schedule.[5] Note that candidate Trump was the *closing* keynote.

---

5. https://freedomfest2015.sched.com/grid/

You will also see that three days *before* Trump spoke, I was the *opening* keynote.

After I spoke, Maria Butina approached me (she had landed in Vegas that morning). She said she was the leader of a Russian group resembling our NRA, and wanted to talk.

What Maria did not know was that of 2,000 people in the room that day, I was the least interested in guns. I have a couple, I keep proficient, but I see them as tools, not something to fetishize. So I brushed Maria off.

Maria came up the next day, told me she had a message for me from Russia, and asked if I would take a ninety-minute meeting the next day. I accepted.

In the first forty-five minutes we were together, I realized that Maria was a remarkable woman. She had a degree in political science, superb knowledge of Russian and American history and literature, and knew our Constitution's intellectual history better than most Americans by a long shot. We had a conversation ranging from Dostoyevsky's *Notes from Underground* to Chekhov's social comedies (some of which I had seen performed in London while a student at Cambridge), Marx and Lenin, Mises, Hayek and the Austrian School, Milton Friedman and Ron Paul.

I happen to remember that I shared with Maria my theory of the Russian Orthodox Church. When the Ottomans took Constantinople, the Orthodox Church fell under Ottoman rule and began paying the *jizya* expected of all non-Muslims. After some years, in order to break away from Ottoman rule the Bishop of Kiev gathered the wealth of his people and paid to the Ottoman Sultan a sum equivalent to thirty or forty years' *jizya*.

Newly freed from the Orthodox Church that remained under Ottoman rule, Russian Orthodoxy developed a theology sharing the traditional Judeo-Christian story: mankind was once on high with God, then experienced the Fall, and we earn our way back to salvation. In some Christian denominations salvation is a personal matter, for some it occurs collectively. The Russian Orthodox tradition is unusual in that while it sees the salvation of mankind as something that happens collectively, *it sees that salvation as something specifically purchased*

*through the enormous capacity of the Russian people to suffer and
endure.*

I told Maria I thought it was convenient for Russian tyrants to have
a church teaching this. Maria seemed surprised I knew such things, as
I was she knew Mark Twain.

Maria gave me to understand she was known across the Russian
power structure, both Kremlin and oligarchy. I could share many
examples, but best would be her relationship to General Mikhail
Kalashnikov, who is a mythical figure to Russians. Kalashnikov was a
WWII soldier who went to work in an arms factory, designing a weapon
released in 1947: hence its name, "Kalishnikov's Automatic-47" (in
Russian: "Avtomat Kalashnikova-47"). The "AK-47." To Russians, the
AK-47 is "The Gun That Freed the World."

At age ninety-three, Kalashnikov had started a gun rights organization in Russia and named twenty-three-year-old Maria to be its president. The fact that ninety-three-year-old General Mikhail Kalashnikov
had selected twenty-three-year-old Maria Butina to be the leader of his
organization meant something to me. Maybe that's because of my relationship with Milton Friedman, of which Maria was aware, or General
Vessey, of which Maria was not.

Maria said she had been sent to America hoping to be a force for
peace by doing what she called "citizen diplomacy". She would live
with her Republican boyfriend in DC and go to graduate school, but
she and Senator Torshin (her "mentor," she said) had decided she
should be building relations in Hillary, Cruz, Rubio, and Trump camps,
so that whoever won the election the next year, Russia would have a
back-channel relationship into the administration.

Maria invited me to fly to Moscow and give a talk on Bitcoin to the

Russian Central Bank, then head to a private meeting for three days in a resort in the Altai with forty-five people from across the Russian power structure. She told me that when I landed in Moscow, Russian FSB (née "KGB") would pull me aside to question me, and counseled me to be honest but not elaborative, and everything would be worked out by the people inviting me.

I don't mean to pretend that stuff happens to me every day, but in the context of my life, it is not as strange as it may sound.

As I explained earlier, I held a security clearance because of my need to receive briefings to perform other peace-related tasks. Because I held that clearance, I had an obligation to report Maria's invitation. In addition, I was 60 percent optimistic: as I said, I have played a tiny role in a handful of peace events and stranger things have happened. But I was 30 percent concerned there was a high-speed Russian woman connected to the Russian oligarchy and FSB planning on swanking around our DC political class.

There was an additional 10 percent reason I will explain later.

My report of our meeting reached DC in hours. Later I was informed it reached all players and was a red flare over Washington that very evening.

The significance of that is as follows: in that famous July 2015 moment when candidate Donald Trump was taking questions from an audience in Las Vegas, and he called on Maria Butina, the federals already knew all about Maria. Two days earlier they had received word from me, and my report had shot around Washington.

I *promise*, when Maria stood up and asked Donald Trump that question, there were federals all over her. July *2015*, not 2016.

That's why you say Durham skipped the first year of the Russian story.

Exactly.

OK, so after you informed the government, what did they do?

What happened next is that Uncle Sam began acting out-of-character. Although I normally did not work with those kinds of federals, a message from me such as that would normally receive significant curiosity. Instead, for two months I only got replies along the lines: *We are not sure if there is anything to this, we are not sure if you should see Maria again or go to Russia, it's up to you, maybe you should but we don't really know.*

Normally in such circumstances, Uncle Sam is not is wishy-washy. I promise.

Eventually I finally let them know: "I am not seeing Maria unless you folks use the word 'greenlight' with me."

I got back a simple message: "Greenlight."

So you saw Maria again.

Yes.

And it turned romantic.

Yes.

Whose idea was that?

Not sure, but once I saw her again, it happened in five seconds. Maybe three.

I should explain something: Maria Butina is a superhuman. In Russian, every year they test all six-year-olds for mental and physical superiority and select the top (0.001%) of children to go to a special school that's a holdover from the Soviet era. At six, Maria was selected for that school, attended for a decade, graduated #2.

Maria is a brainiac. If you want to know how smart Maria is, download an app called "Lumosity" and get the paid (harder) version. Our love notes back-and-forth were our daily scores: she used it a few times then every day among millions of users Maria scored >99 percent.

In addition, Maria was the Greater Moscow Women's Powerlifting Champion. She was also a ferocious kickboxer. And I've seen her get on a treadmill and run hard at a steady speed for sixty minutes, with perfect form throughout, like the Terminator.

My point being, Maria Butina could take care of Maria Butina, don't worry.

So how did the relationship develop?

At the end of the weekend, I suggested to Maria that any time she was bored of her Republican boyfriend she should give me a call, we would pick a city she wanted to see, Miami, San Francisco, New York, wherever, I would send her a ticket and we would meet for a three–four-day tryst there. I give great tryst. I have no Act III whatsoever, but I have a great Act I and Act II. So I told her we'd meet for occasional trysts. I wanted to see her again, naturally. But it would also give me a way to keep tabs on her, and (though I did not tell her this) to get to know her in preparation for perhaps opening doors she wanted opened. Not into politics, but to the thinker-bees… And lastly, for reasons that you will soon understand, I wanted to see what they would do with Maria.

And you were reporting all of this to the FBI?

Yes. I was told that my chain-of-command on this Maria matter was the FBI head of Counterespionage, who reported to the head of Counter-Intelligence, reporting to the National Security Division, reporting to the Executive Assistant Director, reporting to Director Comey.

So you two began having an affair, while she was reporting to the Russian government, and you were to the US government?

Yes. In the context of my life, which Uncle Sam knows down to every tick-and-jottle, none of this is strange. But I grant it may seem strange.

But you do realize that some people will think it not "strange" but "sinister"?

Yes. Withhold judgment. I had ulterior motives you do not know yet.

By November–December 2015 I knew what they were doing. Maria had met with and checked off someone in Hillary's circle (and it turned out later, the federals then gave a prophylactic briefing to Hillary to keep Maria away). But she was still pursuing Cruz, Rubio, and Trump. The federals were letting it happen.

They knew of Maria's meetings, often before they happened, from me. For example, candidate Chris Christie sent me word that he wanted to meet me in New Hampshire. The Federals told me to bring Maria to the meeting. "When she reports it, your stock go up in Moscow will go up," they said. So I picked her up from New York and whisked her to New Hampshire by helicopter. I met with Christie for an hour, bringing Maria in for the last few minutes. Later I was told they used that to get a FISA on Christie. Anyone who met Maria more than glancingly, they could get a warrant on, along with anyone *they* know. Two hops.

In another case, Maria's pillow talk was that some powerful Republicans were trying to arrange a meeting between Don Jr. and herself. There was going to be a conference in the South (either about guns or a Christ). Don Jr. would be at that conference. On Sunday at

2:30 p.m. Don Jr. was to be taken down the rear elevator of his hotel and snuck into a car to take him across town to Maria's hotel, where they would meet for one hour.

I asked FBI, "How should I disrupt this? Whisk her off to the Bahamas?"

To my amazement they said, *Let it play.*

That's why you say the government "began acting out of character"?

Precisely. Normally there would be no way the FBI would let that play.

Incidentally, in the end both Maria and Don Jr. attended a small dinner with a dozen people, but Maria's private meeting with Don Jr. did *not* happen.

By November 2015 I knew we were manufacturing a scandal on the Republican Party. I mentally called it, "Can-O'-Russia-Scandal." It was going to sit on the shelf until they needed it, and when they needed it, they would take it off that shelf, shake it up, crack it open, and spray scandal all over the Republican Party. I thought they were acting funny in July, August, September, and October 2015. By November 2015, around Thanksgiving, I *knew* that is what we were doing.

That is when they came to me one day and said, "We have something more important for you to work on. FBI needs your help setting up Hillary Clinton for a bribe."

They walked me through the principles distinguishing a sting from entrapment. This occurred around Thanksgiving, 2015, in a room with two federal agents. I maintain this is essentially word-for-word what they said to me:

Patrick, there are two groups in the FBI investigating Hillary Clinton. There is one group looking into Secretary Clinton's emails. We all know that's a whitewash. But a group of agents in New York City are looking into her finances, and they really want to get her.

An undercover cop can't just walk down the street, go up to a stranger, and say, "Do you want to buy cocaine?" That would be entrapment: the target would have been drawn into a trap of committing a crime that he probably otherwise would not have committed.

We can't have police running around creating crimes that would not otherwise occur, Patrick. So instead, a prosecutor needs to be able to show that the accused already had a prior disposition to buy cocaine. The prosecutor demonstrates that by proving that the person had already performed one or more predicate acts, such as, "He pulled his car over at a street corner known for drug distribution, he put his car in park, he rolled down his window…" These predicate acts demonstrate that the accused already had a prior disposition to buy the cocaine, and so when the undercover cop approached and sold it to him it was not entrapment, but a crime that was going to happen anyway. So it is a good bust.

Director Comey has been blocking "use of aggressive investigative techniques" (i.e., stings) on Secretary Clinton, because he says that there are insufficient predicate acts to establish that Secretary Clinton has a prior disposition to accept a bribe.

We caught eyes as he said that, because we all read the newspaper and it seemed hard to believe, but I said nothing.

The agent continued: *Recently information has come in that Hillary has accepted a large bribe from a foreign government.*

They told me who did it and how it was done, then said: *The New York FBI agents had leveraged that information as the predicate act to force Comey to sign off on setting Hillary up in a bribery-sting.*

Those New York agents were asking for my help. It was believed that Azerbaijan (a country to which I had never previously traveled) wanted to bribe Hillary in return for having Hillary pledge what one aspect of what her stance towards Azerbaijan would be.

My tasking was as follows:

Mr. Byrne, you are going to create the following end-state: Somewhere in the world there is going to be a room. Secretary Clinton is going to step into that room, and the bagman from Azerbaijan is going to step into that room. They are going to spend ten minutes alone together in that room. Then they will leave separately. You have two months to make that happen anyway you want, Patrick.

I told them I thought it was dicey. USG and I always did business on a handshake (I always said "the fewer pieces of paper between us the better"). But now I was tasked with getting inside a federal election and bribing a presidential candidate. I said it was that rare request for which I'd need one of their "Acts Otherwise Illegal" letters (which are letters they can give you if, as the name suggests, you are asked to do something that is otherwise illegal).

They said they would go discuss it with their bosses.

Days later we met again. An agent said: "We've been instructed to tell you that you cannot be *given* a letter, but if you'll come to DC the Director says you can be *shown* a letter."

I asked, "This is coming from Director Comey?"

Both Special Agents began nod-coughing into their fists as they also glanced and pointed up to the ceiling, while still coughing into their fists.

I asked, "The Director and…. the President?"

They held my eyes, coughed into their hands, and nodded together.

I thought for a few moments then said, "OK, you can tell Director Comey and President Obama that a" (I nodded-coughed into my hand as they had) "from them is good enough for me. Consider Hillary bribed."

Just like that? You agreed?

Yes, I did. And I will refrain from explaining how one goes to a place like Azerbaijan, schmoozes to find the right people, leads them to believe you are the kind of man who can and will do things like that, impresses their bagman, etc. But I promise you, seven weeks later, on January 14, 2016, Hillary knowingly met the bagman in a Washington, DC hotel room.

It worked like this: Hillary was on, say, the 8th floor of the hotel, her assistant was on the 5th, and she had a limousine at 9 a.m.

At 8:30 the bagman entered Hillary's hotel and went up to her assistant's room on 5.

At 8:47 Hillary left the 8th floor and took the elevator from 8th towards Ground, but popped off at 5th and went to her assistant's room. Her assistant stepped out and waited outside the door as Hillary and the bagman spent ten minutes together alone in that room.

Then Hillary came out, took the elevator to the lobby, and left in her limo at 9:02.

It does not show up in her schedule, but that is how it was done. January 14, 2016.

Days later I met with the agents. I thought they might show personality at last. They were always professional with me and had never disclosed political inclination. They knew I am "libertarian republican," but we never touched upon politics. I tried to hold myself to the same ethic that military officers and federal officers do, separating my political thoughts from my job. Or my avocation, in this case. Still, I thought they might surprise me. I didn't expect them to have a bottle of champagne, but I expected smiles.

Instead, the agents were sterner than I had ever seen them. They did not say whether Hillary had taken the bribe. Instead they said, "Patrick, this mission has been re-analyzed, and it has been scrubbed. We need you to forget every moment of it. We mean it. You must erase every moment of this from your memory."

They explained in nervous tones: *This has all been looked at again. Hillary Clinton is going to be our next president, nothing can stop that now. The day she becomes president she is going to do is send her people over to FBI to find out who was part of investigating her, and we are all going to be destroyed. That includes us and chain-of-command. It includes you too, Patrick. So this mission has been scrubbed from the highest levels.*

They sat back and gauged my reaction. It floored me, but I agreed to forget it.

I went home but it did not sit well with me. They could have performed their analysis before tasking me. Their panic seemed feigned. And odd as it sounds, it was unfair to Democrats: we had spent the '90s with a Democrat White House in perpetual investigation, and the right thing to do was to let them pick a clean candidate and not repeat the '90s.

In early February 2016, I met with the two FBI agents again. They brought a third agent, for the following reason. They said that in 2008 a law was passed that made it possible, under certain circumstances, for the Director of Central Intelligence to sign a piece of paper and take over the FBI. Director Brennan had done that on matters relating to Russia. So the DCI would be driving the FBI. They did not say exactly when Brennan had signed that, but they may have indicated it was some months earlier.

I previously said that I had never had anything to do with the CIA because in 1988 I had been identified to Soviet KGB as doing a humanitarian favor for the USG in Vietnam. But I understated it: I had a red line, and that is, I would *never* work with the CIA. I was interested in tasks involving peace, and that was inconsistent with snooping for them. So it was always part of my understanding with USG that nothing I was involved in had CIA involvement.

But here was an odd situation: The *CIA* was not involved; they were nowhere to be seen. In fact, I sensed the CIA was deliberately being kept away from it. But the *Director* of the CIA was now giving orders to the FBI, which had just had me set up a "Can-O'-Russia-Scandal," and had just had me bribe Hillary Clinton then tell me to forget about it.

And now the go-between for James Comey and John Brennan was sitting with us.

I let them know that their explanation as to why I needed to forget it did not sit well with me. And after some hemming and hawing, this is what I finally was given to understand in that first week of February 2016, from three federal agents:

*What's going on, Patrick, is that at this point President Obama has his people across the federal bureaucracy, but especially the Department of Justice. Hillary **is** going to be president for eight years and nothing is going to stop that. But while she's president think of there as being a "Bunsen burner" within the DOJ, and the evidence about the bribe is going to be sitting on that Bunsen burner. The hand on that Bunsen burner is going to be of one of President Obama's people. If Secretary*

Clinton is a good girl, defends Obamacare and such, that flame will stay on "Low". If she is a bad girl, if she starts thinking for herself, that hand [mimes twisting a dial] will turn the Bunsen burner to "High." That way, for the eight years she is president, Hillary Clinton is going to be managed by Barack Obama. Then she is going to step down, and Michelle is going to run ...And Patrick, that's the plan.

Later I learned that the name of the plan was "Operation Snow Globe." Hillary was to spend eight years as president in a Snow Globe that Brennan, Comey, and Obama could shake up anytime they wanted.

I never disclosed this before, but a further thing was said. One of the agents quietly leaned in and added, "So what we are saying, Patrick, is that when we tell you that you must scrub every second of this from that memory of yours, it's really... a matter of life and death."

But he did not *quite* say, "life-and-death." Instead, he said, "...you have to scrub every second of this from that memory of yours, it's really ... a matter of life and d-----" then nodded his head on the last beat completing the sentence. I nodded it back him. We locked eyes, and he raised an eyebrow an almost imperceptible amount to see if I got it. I gave a tiny blink. He leaned back, sad but satisfied. The two other federal agents stared at their shoes.

I wish to be clear that none of them thought this was copacetic. Their delivery was not proud or tough-guy, not, "That's just the way it's going to be, Motherfucker." Just the opposite. Behind their gruff MIB-exteriors they were ashamed. They spoke in a matter-of-fact and measured fashion, with pauses for me to catch up, but with an air of sad finality, as if to say, *it would help if you just accept this, because we're all in the deep end together.* They were family men, and my strong suspicion is that their lives and families were being threatened as well.

They looked like they dreaded delivering me that message.

Now in case you are wondering: You may *think* you've lived, I thought *I* had lived… but you've *never* lived until you've had the liaison from FBI Director James Comey to CIA Director John Brennan sit in a room telling you that you just took part in a soft-*coup*, Obama versus Hillary, Obama is going to be president for twenty-four years, and if you open your mouth you are going to be killed. All as two other FBI agents sit looking at their shoes.

Immediately I flashed back almost exactly ten years, to a late summer day, 2006, when some Senate institutionalists asked me for a favor.

* * * * * *

Byrne is walking along the C&O Canal, on a path he says he used to run in high school. He has been talking of coaches and teachers, his upbringing, his life. He warns that what he is about to explain will sound odd. When told he already crossed that Rubicon, he laughs and promises that, no, only now does the story get truly odd, in two more installments.

Byrne reminds this magazine that when he told us of his fight with Wall Street 2005–2008, he had described Washington, DC, as "turtles all the way down," his metaphor for a stack of compromised institutions.

Now he informs us that he left out something big: the Senate Judiciary Committee. They found him, he says, came to understand that he was correct about Wall Street and DC, and put him to work. Byrne explains how it happened.

According to Byrne, in 2005 Senator Orrin Hatch called to invite Byrne for a walk. Overstock.com was in Salt Lake City, and Hatch was on a visit to his home state. "We had met in the past," says Byrne, "and he had visited Overstock once. It was an unusual for a senator to call insisting I go for a walk with him, but of course I switched my schedule."

At some point in their walk, Byrne says, Hatch said he had come to learn Byrne had an unusual relationship with the United States Government. He asked Byrne to confirm it. "I told him I didn't know what he was talking about. Which led to a second invitation."

"On the next walk, Hatch again confronted me about his understanding that I had some kind of unusual relationship with the US government, and this time cited specifics. I would have just kept on lying, but this was an imposing senator who reminded me of his seniority on various oversight committees of government. Eventually, I acknowledged he was correct."

"Hatch immediately turned on his heel, continued the walk, and it was a settled matter between us." Byrne adds with a chuckle. "Hatch was a shrewd man. He played that perfectly. Looking back, he was chopping off an avenue of retreat for me, a chance for me to equivocate. Then as we walked, he said one specific thing, which I remember because Arlen Specter repeated it when we met."

What did he say?

He said, "Patrick, they say you are a fellow who does... extreme things... to accomplish *whatever* he is asked to accomplish."

Why had he heard that about you?

[Byrne reflects for some moments before answering.]

There were a handful of times I was tasked to accomplish something they did not have a method to accomplish themselves given their rules, they told me, but they would turn a blind eye if I would do it for them.

I would go and do it. They'd be happy until they found out how I did it, and then they would lose their shit. "You did *what*? *What?!?!* Do you have any idea how many rules you broke?" That happened occasionally. Hatch may have heard about that.

In any case, Senator Hatch asked me to meet with Senate Judiciary Committee staffers to present the same evidence I had brought to that stack of "turtles all the way down," which is to say the rest of DC. Evidence the Wall Street settlement system had cracks, bad guys had figured out how to game the cracks to steal billions, it was harming investors, corporate voting, and would destabilize the financial system (as Greenspan would testify to Congress three years later, during the 2008 financial crisis). I had figured it out in 2005 and had brought data, economists, and whistleblowers to the SEC, FINRA, NASD, Senate Banking, House Financial Services... They had listened politely, or impolitely, then shut the door.

So Hatch had me bring to the Judiciary Committee those same data, economists, and whistleblowers we had brought elsewhere in DC to no avail. After two to three meetings the Judiciary folks said, "'Yep, you're right. Clearly that's illegal and harms the market. Now let's talk about who you have been bringing this information to and what their responses were.'"

Eventually they explained: The Senate Judiciary Committee is the ultimate protector of the Constitution, Patrick. That is because we investigate corruption. Our mandate to investigate corruption transcends every other power within government. If we suspect there is corruption in the manufacture of nuclear weapons, for example, we investigate it, and nobody tells the Judiciary Committee that we don't have proper clearances. Our powers transcend everything in government because we investigate corruption, and corruption is anything that can be "touched by a civil or criminal penalty." Which is every aspect of life. Which means, Patrick, the Judiciary Committee investigates anything in the USA it wants to investigate.

So lawyers who worked with me began interacting with them on these issues. They had us meeting with various officials in the SEC, DOJ, and regulatory bodies, and then reporting back to them about those officials. Frankly, they had us do that within Congress itself.

After some months, I was told to bring two insiders to meet Senate Judiciary Committee Chairman Arlen Specter. What I knew of Chairman Specter was that he had been a Democrat federal prosecutor in Pennsylvania, was elected to the House as a Democrat, and then to the Senate, but somewhere along the way he transitioned to being a Republican. However, before we met, I was told he was in the process of de-transitioning back to Democrat, though I don't remember if that was public yet.

I brought two deep-inside Wall Street insiders from Staten Island. Specter spent fifteen–twenty minutes listening to them, indicated he understood what they had told him, believed it, and turned to me.

Chairman Specter was going through cancer treatments. His hair was wispy from chemotherapy, and he had gauze on the right side of his throat with access to a vein, just as I had lived with on-and-off for three years. We spoke of cancer, and then my life.

It was a strange conversation. I thought we would be talking about things like Wall Street's Option Market Maker Exemption. Instead, he had me walk through my background, my upbringing, and even asked if I had had a religious upbringing. I told him that I tend to describe my teenage years as, "I majored in Catholic and minored in Jew, but by the time I went to college I had become a Seeker." He was Jewish and thought that was funny.

Bizarrely, Specter asked if I had been an altar boy. I told him that I had indeed been until age 14, a bit unusually late. I happen to remember that distinctly, because in thirty years I don't think it had come up in conversation, or even crossed my mind. In all my life it has come up in two conversations, and the first was this conversation with Specter.

After more an hour, the meeting ended. As he stood to leave, Chairman Specter leaned over and said something personal to me. He told me that when he had been a federal prosecutor in Philadelphia, psychologically the toughest cases to investigate and prosecute were cases involving corruption. That was because, Specter said, "Over time, you start to feel like an enemy of your own government, and of your own country."

I was perplexed Specter said that. I surmised he was referring to articles I had been penning and interviews I was giving discussing Wall Street's "regulatory capture" of the SEC.

Only much later did I understand why Chairman Specter said that to me as we parted. He was considering asking me to do something, and his purpose in meeting me was to size me up. He had decided to go forward with me. His story from his days as a federal prosecutor was a warning he was giving me to accompany the request he knew he would soon be making.

But now I must laugh at the irony. DHS is now telling trainees that I am DHS Domestic Threat #1. So Chairman Specter's observation has come true.

Byrne says that a month later, he received a call asking him to come to DC. "Don't bring anyone, don't bring any lawyers," that is to say, those colleagues who had been accompanying him on previous visits to the Senate Judiciary.

Byrne went alone to DC and at the appointed hour went to the appointment. He walked into a room and found seven Senators from both parties, waiting. Byrne describes what happened next.

Arlen Specter, Democrat-turned-Republican-Now-Detransitioning-to-Democrat, was there and chaired the meeting. Patrick Leahy of Vermont (Democrat) was part of this, but he showed up a few minutes late. The junior Democratic senator from another New England state was there, medium height, slim, solid, standing erect like a general (because I am not 100 percent certain of the name I am not identifying him, but in my mind I can still see his posture and am 100 percent confident that it was a Democrat junior senator from New England).

There was also mention of another Democrat. The name "Ted Kennedy" was spoken, but he was not there, and I did not catch if they were saying, "He is with this but could not be here," or were saying, "We tried to get him to agree but in the end we could not."

On the Republican side there were Senators Hatch, Grassley, and Crapo. There was also Senator Kit Bond, who was Chairman of Senate Intelligence.

We never sat down. These Senators huddled around me as Chairman Specter repeated what I had been told all year, that Senate Judiciary is the ultimate bulwark protecting the Constitution because its mandate includes stopping corruption, and therefore our power transcends every other power within government.

Then Specter said, "We think you are right. There is some kind of corrupt force taking over our government. Some days it is like a foreign country doing it, other days not. It's everywhere. It's our job to stop but we can't stop it. We've seen that…" As he continued, I momentarily lost track as waves of relief washed over me. Until then, everyone had acted like they thought I was a nut to be telling them there were cracks in Wall Street's settlement system, billions or trillions were being stolen, it would all melt down, and the SEC was asleep at the switch or else captured by the financial industry it was supposed to regulate. In 2005, newspapers had run photos of me with UFO's coming out of my head simply to suggest that Wall Street had captured the SEC. It was 'conspiracy theory,' they said.

But now, after eighteen months of banging my head on DC, the Senate Judiciary from both sides of the aisle had looked at the same data and listened to the same whistleblowers and insiders, and decided I was correct. Not just about Wall Street mischief, but also about the impression I was forming of Washington, DC.

It was like surfacing after a long swim underwater.

Finally, I interrupted Chairman Specter to gasp, "I know! I know! This is what *I've* been saying. How can you even *stop* something like that?"

Specter said, "We're going to stop it because we have *you* and *you're* going to stop it."

Hatch added, "That's why you're here." The other senators around piled-on, saying, "Yeah yeah, that's why *you're* here."

They told me that the country needed me to disrupt that corruption taking over the United States Government. They did not know how, they told me, and they said they might not be Senators when I finished, might not even be *alive* when I finished. But the country needed me to make this project my mission in life.

Oddly, no one *asked* me anything. No one said, "Would you be willing to do this?" They simply told me the country needed me to do it so that is what I was going to do.

Byrne was forty-three and says that having seven US Senators from both parties standing around him telling him these things was disorienting and intimidating.

Specter said, "We're going to be with the President tomorrow night, and we're going to show him a letter that is going to be sitting the rest of your life in a safe in DC." He held up a letter that was on Senate Judiciary Committee stationary. I reached as if to take it, but another Senator shouted, "He cannot touch it!" So Hatch held it, and I bent with my hands clasped behind my back and scanned it for fifteen seconds. It was about one-and-a-half pages long.

Byrne says that the first paragraph spoke to the Judiciary Committee's concern over, "systemic corruption infiltrating the federal institutions of our nation's government." He says the second paragraph opened with words along the following lines: "The United States Senate Committee on the Judiciary requests that Patrick Byrne be afforded extraordinary latitude under the laws of the United States of America to investigate and disrupt corruption within the government."

I was flabbergasted. After scanning the letter for fifteen seconds, the senators—either from noticing the confusion on my face or simply because they were senators—started talking to me, at which point I could no longer read.

Chairman Specter said, "This is not a *pardon*, you can't go *kill* anyone, but short of that, this is going to make it very unlikely any prosecutor ever touches you."

I looked away from the letter and straightened up to his face as he continued, "We get that you're a bit different, Patrick, we get that you're a horse of a different color..."

The other Senators broke out in guffaws, "You sure are a horse of a different color!" and one made cuckoo motions with his finger around his ear, making everyone laugh.

"But we've come to know you, Patrick, and ...we love you. We really love you."

Seven senators stood around me nodding, "Yeah we really love you, Patrick."

Chairman Specter ended, telling me that the country needed me to do this with my life, so that is what I was going to do.

I pondered for perhaps five seconds, then asked one question: "No takebacks?"

Seven senators stood around me laughing and saying, "*Hahaha* no takebacks very funny *haha* no takebacks no takebacks!"

I thought, then answered, "Gentlemen... What can I say? I won't let you down."

I then shook hands and had a word with each senator.

Senator Grassley and I stood talking about his involvement in the matter of SEC whistleblower Gary Aguirre: Grassley seemed surprised and pleased that I knew about it and stood looking up at me grinning from ear to ear.

One of the senators told me that this had not been done in sixty-five years, but that during World War II there was a concern over German sympathizers within our government so a Wall Street man with contacts in government was asked to "become" a German sympathizer to flush the others out. This story may have come from the Democratic senator from New England, of whom I have a clear visual memory from his build and formal posture.

Senator Crapo (my height) stood facing me waiting for me to say something, and I waited for him to something, until finally I just repeated, "Sir, I won't let you down."

Chairman Kit Bond from Senate Intelligence Committee was there to endorse the project. As we stood facing each other shaking hands, I took note of what a large, broad man he was, with big meaty hands, like he had once been a farmer or laid bricks for a living.

Senator Leahy and I spoke last. He apologized for having been late, saying he was running between votes but wanted to make sure he let me know he endorsed this. I thanked him and told him of my favorite moment in life, the one that will flash before my eyes as I die: I was nineteen, alone, tapping 400 maple trees on a Vermont hillside, while Stubby Fullerton's sugar-shack up the road spewed caramelized apple-wood smoke, filling the Kedron Valley.

Byrne says this conversation happened in September 2006, on what he describes as an Indian summer's day in Washington, DC. Asked if he knows how unlikely the story sounds, Byrne replies:

"Yes, I do," says Byrne. "It probably checks all the boxes on mega-lomania with delusions of grandeur. All I can say is: It happened."

Byrne mentions claims that journalists Matt Taibbi of *Rolling Stone* and Sheilah Kolhaktar of the *New Yorker* have spoken with staffers from the 2006 Judiciary Committee who confirmed that in the 2006 files of the Senate Judiciary Committee there is indeed a bizarre letter concerning Byrne. Byrne claims that Trey Gowdy knows about the letter, for reasons Byrne will not explain.

Byrne says that early in 2023 someone he knows was visiting

Grassley and asked about the letter, and that Grassley laughed and laughed, saying, "Yes we know Patrick, yes we remember that conversation, yes we are holding the letter." Byrne says that he has also heard that the DOJ has been wanting to indict him, but that Senate Judiciary has made it clear that it would be a "party foul," as Byrne calls it.

* * * * * *

But that is all from 2006. Now let us flash-forward almost precisely 10 years, to February 2016 where we left off the story.

Please do. Where were we?

We were in a room with three federal agents who used me to set up a fake Russian scandal on the Republicans, and then had me facilitate a bribe for Hillary Clinton then told me it would be used to blackmail her for eight years until Michelle could be installed, and then told me I would be killed if I opened my mouth. Can we pick up there?

OK. I'm tracking. Go ahead.

Yes. So in early February 2016, I figured out that I had being unwittingly used by the National Security apparatus in domestic political espionage. I knew with 98 percent confidence that they were using me to manage Maria to smudge up the Republican Party, and that someday they would pull the pin on that hand-grenade and a massive Russia Scandal would blow up on Republicans. In addition, three federal agents had also had me set up an $18 million bribe for Hillary Clinton for purposes of a sting, but afterwards I learned that we had set up Hillary not for law enforcement purposes, but so that she could be blackmailed by Obama to keep her under his thumb until Michelle could be installed.

Now, I know that though those names were used with me, it does not mean much. That world is such a Hall of Mirrors. There are people in that world whose names do not appear on an organization chart anywhere. Whoever was behind this political espionage, for convenience let us call them, the Deep State". The Deep State tricked me into bribing Hillary Clinton so she could be blackmailed. The Deep State tricked me into helping them use Maria to set up a "Can-o'-Russia-Scandal" to spray over the Republican Party. And then they threatened my life if I opened my mouth about any of it.

Someday I'll tell this to 12 other citizens, good and true. So I ask: Does that sound like 'systemic corruption infiltrating the federal institutions of our nation's government'?

Byrne seems genuinely curious. He is told that, if his story is true, it would indeed count as "systemic corruption infiltrating the government." Byrne seems relieved.

That's good, because I decided to avail myself of "extraordinary latitude under the laws of the United States of America."

I decided to derail the *coup*... the moment I got a kill shot.

"The moment you got a kill shot"? What do you mean?

My Rabbi taught me this approach to life. Let me give you an example. My brother Mark was running a hedge fund, and Buffett put a lot of money into it. At one point Mark did a certain trade that Buffett liked, and he told Mark to lay it on big. Their prime broker, a large Wall Street bank, knew it was Buffett because of the scale, and took advantage by front-running the trade. It cost Buffett $100 million.

Mark was angry, but Buffett told him not to be. He said, "When things like this happen, Mark, don't get angry. We're not going to say anything, we're going to wait for an opportunity, and then we're going to really *fuck* them." They waited until there was an even larger trade to put on, and Buffett had my brother place a small version of the trade with that bank, but *opposite* of what he really planned to do. The bank front-ran it again, loading up on a position they thought they would be selling Buffett. Instead, Buffett had Mark place through another big bank his real *huge* trade in the opposite direction, and by the time the first crooked bank figured it out it had lost $600 million to Buffett.

That is how my rabbi teaches brokers not to game his trading.

I had been used to bribe and blackmail Hillary Clinton, the likely next president. I had been used to manufacture a scandal linking Republicans to Russia. And whoever was behind it all had ordered my handlers to threaten my life to keep me silent.

Was I going to run to Loretta Lynch about all this? Yeah, that's funny.

So I decided I was going to lay low, and when the right moment came and the universe gave me a shot, I was going to derail the *coup* by *fucking* everybody involved.

Because of your letter? That's hard to believe.

Well, you have not read that letter.

If you are suggesting that there might have been emotion attached to my decision, you may be correct. The *logic* of it was the letter. The Senate Judiciary Committee told me our country was being taken over through some kind of corruption of our federal institutions, and they were asking me to stop it. So once the phonies of the Russian investigation become apparent to me, and then especially once the Bunsen Burner was revealed to me, I had a duty to act.

But yes, there was also emotion involved. One federal agent

representing James Comey and John Brennan had threatened my life. Two other FBI agents heard it and looked at their shoes. As I said, they were aghast, like the same threat had been made against all of them, with a message to deliver it to me.

But frankly, I think they may have looked aghast because they thought it was a bad idea. Let me explain: such meetings are practically handcrafted. Before they meet with you, every aspect of the meeting has been scripted. Rehearsed, I think. There are shrinks back at HQ who know everything about you, who know you better than you know yourself. I am confident that when asked, those psychologists said some version of: *This guy is as Irish as Paddy's Pig. Don't threaten him. It will be counterproductive.* Such people know to avoid threatening Irishmen or Sicilians, that you deal with them in other ways. Anyone who is street knows Irishmen and Sicilians respond poorly to being threatened. It's an honor thing. If someone threatens you and you take it, then you walk around the rest of your life as a punk. It is better to die than to be that kind of a man. As an Arab once said to me. "A man without honor is a dead man anyway." That sums it up.

These agents knew me. *Had* known me for years. I could tell they hated what they were doing, or thought it was a truly bad idea. Probably both.

[Byrne explains that given the Hillary-Bribery-and-Bunsen-Burner story, the Russian "Can-O'-Scandal" setup, and the fact that his chain-of command had just threatened his life over (he senses) the objection of his handlers, he felt confident he had found the "systemic corruption infiltrating our nation's government."]

After a few seconds thinking all that through, I grimaced and said, "Yes, Sir, I understand, I will scrub every trace it from my memory,

I promise…" While on the inside I was thinking, *I will derail these motherfuckers on a world-historic scale… the moment I get a kill-shot.*

How were you planning on doing that?

I did not know. That is what I mean by, "…the moment I get a kill-shot." I was just going to keep my eyes open, and when that opportunity came, derail their plan. In a big way. Bigger than Buffett thinks.

I don't mean to be arrogant but think about it. Who do they think they are, threatening me? I can tell you it was not anyone at the FBI. It was some political flunky somewhere making these calls, someone who is not on an org chart, or maybe someone in the National Security Council, some wannabee gangster who is not in the least bit street or else they would have known (as my handlers did) that threatening my life would be counterproductive.

Which brings us to the fourth and final part of the story. The first three were the setup of a Russian Collusion Delusion, the setup of Hillary's bribe-and-blackmail, and the flashback to the 2006 Senate Judiciary committee assignment to infiltrate and disrupt the Deep State. Now comes the fourth and final part of the story: "The Rape & Murder of Maria Butina."

"The Rape & Murder of Maria Butina"? She wasn't murdered. She is a member of the Russian Parliament today.

I know. She wasn't raped either. It was another setup. Like Hillary's bribe and the Russian Hoax.

I hope you plan on unpacking this.

I told you how the FBI agents had spent ten minutes teaching me about stings, right? How to avoid entrapment, a prosecutor must show that you had committed predicate acts that establish you already had the prior disposition to commit a crime, so when the undercover officer engaged in one with you it is not entrapment, right?

Yes, I remember.

Well at this point in my story, whoever was calling the shots, let me avoid claiming it was Comey or Brennan or Obama because for all I know it was perhaps a "Deep State of people not on any org chart. Well, this Deep State had had me facilitate an $18 million bribe for Hillary to lure her into a Snow Globe. This Deep State had had me get to know Maria not because they were considering having someone meet her, as they had led me to think, but because they were constructing a "'Can-O'-Russia-Scandal'" to shake up, crack open, and spray on the Republicans (primarily Cruz, Rubio, or Trump) any time they wanted. And through my handlers, that same shot-caller had just threatened my life. Would you agree that those predicate acts establish that whoever was at the other end of my chain-of-command had a prior disposition to misuse our national security apparatus for their own private ends?

When you put it that way, I suppose so, yes.

Ok. Then by the power vested in me by the 2006 Senate Judiciary Committee, I decided to disrupt their *coup d'état.*

How did you plan on doing that?

I did not know yet. But I was thinking of a torpedo the USA has in its arsenal. Did you know that if we think there is a Russian sub off our coast, we have a torpedo that we can fly out in an airplane to that patch of ocean? We drop it, it hangs from a parachute, when it splashes down it releases the parachute and activates. Ping! Ping! It listens for the submarine, and when it hears it just homes in on it: ping-PING-**PING**!

I had my finger on the button, and when the Deep State next showed its wake, I was going to lob a torpedo in its direction.

Did the opportunity come?

Yes. Five months later. In the first week of July 2016. For reference, the Republican Convention occurred in the *last* few days of July 2016, but by the *first* few days of July 2016 it was clear that Trump was going to be the nominee. They sent word, we met, and they told me that I had been right about Russia. There were clear signs of Russian operations in the USA, they wished they had listened to me and not had me break up with Maria, and Russia had become the highest-level national emergency. They told me that the United States government normally does not do certain things, *never* does certain things, and this was one of them. I could refuse the tasking, and no one would think less of me. But I was being asked to rekindle a romantic relationship with Maria Butina, get back inside her head, and get to the bottom of anything she knew about Russian activities in the US. John Brennan and James Comey would be personally supervising the mission: the agents would be leaving meetings with me to go back to the office and report over video conference directly to Directors Brennan and Comey.

So I said to myself, "There's my kill shot."

What do you mean?

I saw instantly that I would be setting them up on rape and murder. I would get the information they wanted, but in the process, I would set Comey and Brennan up on rape and murder.

You see, there was so much fake about their requests. How they had had me work Maria, allegedly to learn enough about her so they might agree to open doors for her in the foreign policy establishment. How they had had me breakup on the grounds that they had determined that she was just a normal grad student. How they were now coming back, acting all alarmed at realizing I had been correct, and they should have listened to me…. It was all fake. I knew them asking me to get back with Maria had some purpose *other* than what they were asking me. Nothing was right about the Russian matter, and they told me Brennan was running the Russian matter. Nothing was right about the Hillary matter, and they had told me Comey was behind it. And now Brennan and Comey were both behind this new order which, after all the excuses they had given me to avoid looking at Maria, also seemed fake. It was the opportunity to fire my torpedo for which I had been waiting.

So I decided on the spot I would get the information they wanted: after all, this was national security. But I also decided that this time I wouldn't lay a finger on Maria; I would treat Maria like she was the niece of Czar Nicholas II. I was going to be the most exquisite gentleman imaginable, in a manner that could later be studied by prosecutors and historians. But I would give my chain of command a chance to implicate themselves in rape-and-murder. No one can spin rape-and-murder. As they say at a craps table, "It's a natural winner."

Shall I keep going?

Oh, please do.

I had been a jerk when I broke off with Maria the first time. I was extremely ill. As a matter of fact, back in that winter of 2016, I was Stage IV of two unrelated diseases at the same time. That may be why I got pulled into this: everyone expected me to be dead in months. Including me. So when they told me to break up, I broke up and was abrupt about it because I was so ill.

So it took a couple months to get things rekindled with Maria. Soon we were communicating warmly, and I invited her out to Utah for a four-day weekend including the opening of a new building we had built for our HQ, and our annual corporate party.

Here's the catch. When she arrived, I told her that this time, we were going to have an old-fashioned European courtship. When she visited, she would sleep in the guest room. After six months she would decide if she wanted to be with me, and if she did, she would move to Utah, we would be together, and only then would we sleep together again. She thought it was romantic and, since she was living with a Republican guy, it suited her conscience better. Maria is really quite a decent person.

So we spent three–four days getting reacquainted, going on drives, going to gun stores, and shooting ranges, etc. But keeping things purely Platonic. And she is a great gal with whom to spend time.

[A jogger eyes Byrne in passing. He waits moments before resuming.]

At first opportunity I debriefed with my handlers. I told them I had deliberately gotten Maria inebriated, introduced her to marijuana, then tricked her into smoking an extra-powerful joint that half-knocked her out, questioned her, and could find no discrepancies. Just so you are aware, it is a bit edgy to talk that way regarding activities within the USA. Really, our people are Boy Scouts. It is a disadvantage. Overseas, everyone is always trying to get each other wasted and talk. Maria was always trying to get me drunk and talk. But in the USA, our people don't condone that stuff. So as I said, it was a little edgy to say that I had done it on an assignment within the USA. I could tell it gave the agents pause. But they wrote it down.

Just as I was leaving, they asked if we had been physical again, and I answered with unusual machismo: "Yeah I'm back in the saddle, I shagged her all night long." It was out of character for such talk among us. Nothing like that had ever been said between us. It likely was a mistake. I was aiming to suggest that Maria meant nothing to me, but I probably overdid it: looking back, at least one of them registered a suspicious glance. I had my reasons, as you will see, but I overplayed it a bit.

We met again a week later for a more detailed briefing. I dropped clues that I had mapped out the night before. I did not describe the weekend in an organized manner as I normally would. Instead, I told it in fragments: there was the time we went to the gun range, there was this evening I made lobster linguine, and so forth. But I had designed it so that after I left the debriefing and they spent a few minutes fitting all their notes together, what would emerge would be this picture: on the third day Maria had been with me I had taken her to a gun range, then on a drive, got her inebriated, taken her home, made her a romantic dinner and gotten her further wasted, questioned her for an hour and found no discrepancies... then shagged her.

And there is a word for that, right?

Yes… and it is not a good word.

I know it's not. It is a horrible word. What is it? Say it.

"Sexual assault."

Try "rape." Once they put my clues together, they would report on videoconference to Brennan and Comey that I had gotten Maria Butina drunk, drugged her, then raped her.

Why?

Why? Because I wanted to see what Comey and Brennan would do.

OK, I'll bite: What did Comey and Brennan do?

They did nothing. That's what's so funny.

The next time I met the agents, they had faces set in stone, they hated me … but they had been ordered not to bring the subject up. Clearly in their video conference, Brennan and Comey had heard the previous report and told them, "Agents, don't you say a *goddamned thing* about it. Don't you ask Byrne a follow-up question on it. If Byrne has drugged and raped Maria Butina, so be it. Just let it go, we got more important things going on here. We got a Russian Hoax to set up here. We need Byrne and Maria for that." Get it?

You know something, Patrick? They were right. The Senators who said that you're a horse of a different color, that you're extreme. They had your number.

Yeah, I get that a lot.

So I waited another meeting or two… then I proposed *murdering* Maria Butina.

Actually, I worked it all out then waited until they brought it up again. At one meeting they said, "The folks back East want to know if you can really do this without falling in love."

I told them, word-for-word: "Nietzsche said, 'Philosophers don't really fall in love: it would be like seeing delicate little hands on a Cyclops.' Can you imagine that, a monster with tiny, delicate hands, how silly that would be? You tell the folks back East that if they send word, I'll cut this chick's head off and bury her in the Utah desert, nobody'll know a thing."

I am pleased to report that three federal agents simultaneously jumped from their chairs into gunfighters' crouches. One reached behind his back and I heard a weapon click as it left its holster, but then he reholstered and stood over me in my chair wagging a finger in my face. "Let's get one thing perfectly clear, Byrne. *We don't care* what orders come from DC: If you harm a hair on Maria's head, we're going to kill you ourselves," he barked. All three glanced at each other and nodded curtly to me, suggesting the subject had been discussed.

It was exactly the right thing to say. I am highly confident these agents were not bad men, but like me had been tricked into the situation we were in. Yes, they conveyed a death threat to me, but they were all family men, and I am sure they thought they had no way out themselves. They did not know about my Golden Letter. They worked for bad people, and like me had not realized it. I think we all found out the same day how we had been used.

So I raised my hands up and said to the agents, "Got it, got it. 'No murdering Maria.' I got it." And moved on to the next subject we were there to discuss.

[Byrne catches his breath as we turn back to our parked cars.]

But you see: I had boxed in the Deep State. I had realized that I was on a path working for people, *whoever* they were, who were trying to take over the government of the United States through political espionage. I didn't know who it was, though I knew the names used to get me to play my role. But I knew I had bribed Hillary for what turned out to be blackmail. And I knew I had been used in the setup of a fake Russian scandal. And my life had been threatened if I opened my mouth. That was the path I was on.

So metaphorically speaking, I chopped a tree down across that path. I put whoever was running this soft- *coup d'etat* in the following position: either they had to *stop* the *coup* they were setting up and whatever role they had written for Maria to play in it… or somebody was going to have to sign off on an aggravated-rape-and-possible-murder of a woman they knew to be innocent that never actually happened.

Byrne…. OK, what happened?

Somebody signed off on the aggravated-rape-and-possible-murder of a woman they knew to be innocent that never actually happened. Then they had me "date" her for five more months. *Yuck yuck yuck yuck.*

After five more months she told me she *did* want to move to Utah and be with me. I was told to end it again, on the grounds that, "We are learning so much watching her move around DC, seeing who she is having dinners with…"

So I broke off. Just like that. You get why?

At this point, we're afraid to guess about anything.

Because ultimately, what was my assignment? My real assignment was this: in 2006, 300 million Americans chose a Senate, which chose a Senate Judiciary Committee, which chose a chairman, who told me their power transcended every other power within government, some kind of corrupt force was taking over the US government, it was their job to stop it but they were losing the fight and so they needed me to stop it for them.

So the more corrupt my orders, the better. My Senate assignment demanded I go along with the most corrupt orders to *find* the Deep State. Maria was my perfect opportunity.

Remember how I said that I saw Maria as 60 percent opportunity for good (peace between Russia and the USA), 30 percent risk (because she was swanking around with our DC political class while connected to Russian senators and FSB), and 10 percent something else?

Yes.

That last 10 percent is what I am talking about now.

In high school wrestling and football we used to use plastic mouth-guards. One would drop one into boiling water, bite the soft plastic for a minute, and have a custom mouthguard.

I regret to say that as fond of and impressed with Maria as I was, in a sense she was a plastic mouthguard. By 2015 I had reasons to believe something deeply corrupt was going on within our government. I cannot explain why here, but I had been bumping my head against the Deep State since about 2010. Too many opportunities missed, too many decisions made no sense. I did not know what, exactly, I did not even know how to explain it back then.

But Maria came along and represented a perfect opportunity: she was a blank mouth guard. Maria seems to want to be dropped into the national security pot, so let's do it and see what the Deep State does with her. I knew I would get a dental impression of the Deep State. Which was a perfect way to complete the Senate Judiciary Committee's tasking, and a perfect opportunity to show America what's what.

In other words, when I first reported Maria, 10 percent of me was thinking: "Let's see how they handle this Maria situation. If my hunch is correct, I will end up with a perfect dental impression of the Deep State to show America."

How did it play out?

After they thought I had manipulated, seduced, drugged, raped, formed a plan to murder Maria Butina, and proposed doing it... they thought I was *really* one of their boys. They had me continue seeing her for five months, then break off so she would stay in Washington going out to dinner with Republicans and posting photos of it on Facebook.

Then, fifteen months later, as the Russian Collusion narrative reached a frenzy, around the time the public was starting to ask why this Russian scandal did not seem to have any actual *Russians* in it... the day that Trump and Putin met, just a few hours *before* they met, a CNN van with an FBI SWAT team in tow descended on Maria's boyfriend's DC apartment to televise her arrest.

For the next year, night after night on TV it was photos of "alleged Russian spy Maria Butina," a striking Russian redhead with sniper rifle and thigh-high leather boots. Hollywood's image of a Russian spy.

That clip of "accused spy Maria Butina asking Trump a question in Vegas" played 1,000 times on the news, over and over, associating the two of them.

Eventually a federal prosecutor argued in a courtroom for fifteen years in prison for Maria, on the grounds that grave damage was done to our national security by Maria Butina having those dinners around DC with Republicans and posting photos of them on Facebook... all of them being meetings the Federals knew about, often before they happened, sometimes from me, and occasionally created by me at their request, like the Chris Christie meeting.

From the day Maria arrived in July 2015, it was all as "producer-driven" as the Spice Girls.

A couple years ago in an interview on the Wondery podcast, Peter Strzok said words to this effect: *You really want to know what made us open Crossfire Hurricane in July 2016? We learned about Maria Butina! That's why it started.*

That is a flat lie. They learned about her in July of 2015 and played cat-and-mouse games with her for a year. That's not a theory. I am a participant. A witness. I did it. He is lying. They are lying.

The Senate Intel Report about this is a vacuous nothing-burger. It missed all of this.

The Durham Report gets correct what happened after July 2016 but covers up everything else. Of course, in his four years of "investigation," Durham not only failed to *interview* Strzok, McCabe, Comey, or Brennan, but Durham failed to **subpoena** them. They kept me silent four years telling me they were investigating this story, but then did not even subpoena my chain-of-command. So at the end of the day, his report is a joke.

So… you tricked your chain of command into signing off on rape and murder? Couldn't you have gone with something less horrible?

No no. Rape-and-murder was great. Rape-and-murder was *perfect.*

First, because it was the opportunity that presented itself.

Second, because it was the start of the Weinstein era.

They had been playing games with me since the day I reported Maria. I knew they had me operating within some big con they were playing. I knew they were no-goodnicks, but I could not suss out what they were up to. But after the Hillary bribery-and-blackmail caper I decided that it was up to me to derail them. I did not know how. It was like being the slowest man on a kickoff team, having to make that clutch tackle. Which is something I know about.

So when they came back and asked me to re-seduce Maria, it was a perfect opportunity to create a rape-murder gambit on them: they'd have to sign off to continue what they were engineering.

It was beautiful. You know why? Because it's tough to spin rape and murder. These guys spin everything else. Bribery and laptops and recordings and videotapes... but you can't spin rape-and-murder. It was the opportunity that came along, and it was perfect.

Why aren't you in prison?

Four years ago, I walked into the DOJ and told them all this. The first thing they said was that I was in a lot of trouble if Maria did not corroborate my story. I told them I was not in the least worried, go talk to Maria. They asked how I could be so confident, and I told them that Maria Butina is a Woman of Steel, and no matter that she had been sitting in a box for nine months, had nine more months to go, and knew I had something to do with it all, still she would tell the truth. You'd have to know Maria Butina to understand why I was so confident.

They next day they interviewed Maria in her box. She told them what she told Sara Carter shortly thereafter, when Sara interviewed Maria in prison.

[Byrne switches to a Russian accent]

"Have never met such gentleman as Patrick Byrne! Yes, first time we dated was physical, but second time we dated Patrick was perfect gentleman! I did not understand a man could be so kind. He flew me in helicopters and jets, beautiful restaurants... but he insisted I sleep in guest room. Did not lay finger on me. I did not know such a gentleman still existed!'"

Four years ago the DOJ and Sara Carter confirmed all of this. That first period Maria and I dated was ... *wonderful*. But the second time I treated her as untouchable as a Romanov princess. I just reported crazy shit up my chain of command to see how wed they were to the *coup d'état* we were working on.

You know how wed they were? Turns out they were *rape-and-murder wed*. Turns out, they were so focused on their *coup d'état* they wouldn't let a little aggravated-rape-and-murder get in the way.

Happy Birthday America! There's your Deep State. *Yuck yuck yuck yuck*.

Mission Accomplished.

This story may sound odd to people who do not know me well. But there are probably still dozens of people around DC who knew me in high school. You could ask any one of them, "Is Patrick Byrne the kind of guy who, if he figured out the Directors of the FBI and CIA and possibly the President were running a soft-*coup* to take over the US government, would compromise them in a rape-and-murder setup of his own creation?" I promise, the answer you will get from ten out of ten is, "Yeah that's Pat." Some will say, "You could have told me the story without the name, and I could have told you, 'Oh you're talking about Patrick Byrne, right?'"

Why is that? You think you're a saint?

No not at all. I am the farthest thing from a saint. In fact I'm diabolical. Obviously.

You know, when Gandhi died, Orwell wrote an essay on him, *Notes on Gandhi*. In it he wrote, "Many men do not aspire to be saints, and some who aspire to be saints never felt much temptation to be men." I am no saint.

But it is more that... well you'd have to ask them.

We'd like your thoughts.

[Byrne ponders for some moments]

Remember how I mentioned that the Arlen Specter conversation was the first of two conversations in my life that I had cause to remember I had been an altar boy?

Yes.

The second time was at a dinner I had about fifteen years ago with Susan Sarandon and Tim Robbins. It was a year or two before they split. Halfway through dinner, Tim said something funny to me. He said, "You were an altar boy, weren't you?"

I told him he was correct, and asked how he knew.

He said, "You have a quirkiness about you. Sometimes men who were altar boys have that specific quirkiness, and man, you have it.'"

I told him that many people, including myself, think Tim Robbins is a little quirky.

Tim replied that he had been an altar boy too. He told me that if as I go through life and note men who have that same quirkiness as he and I have, I will generally find that it is men who were altar boys.

Think of Tim Robbins's sense of humor. It is that characteristic. To me, frankly, it is almost *funny* that someone thought they could tell me we just destroyed the USA and I had to keep my mouth shut or be killed, and it would end there with me. Actually, it's *really* funny. [Byrne guffaws.] In fact it's *hilarious*, that someone actually thought that.

That observation about altar boys was a strange one for Tim Robbins to make. But he was right. Smart actors like Tim are astute observers of the human condition.

Anyway... so enough about bribery, blackmail, rape, and murder. If you want to find out who set up RussiaGate, who set up the Hillary Bribery-and-Blackmail Hoax, and who thought it would be productive to send me a death threat, find out who signed off on the rape and murder of Maria Butina so the Russia Hoax project could continue. Find that out and you will find who is behind a lot that has happened since then as well, perhaps.

What do you mean by that?

It moves into the realm of speculation. Let us stick with specific, concrete claims.

OK. What was it like to be proven right in 2008 after three years of press abuse?

There is a Zen story about a monk who loves being a monk. One day a village girl gets pregnant, and she tells town-folk that the monk is the father. The villagers come and berate the monk, "You horrible man. How could we have trusted you around our children?!?"

The monk replies calmly, "Is that so?"

He takes the baby, raises it. From then on, whenever the villagers see him, they always tell him, "We will never forget what you did, you horrible man, we trusted you!"

The monk replies calmly each time, "Is that so?"

After some years, filled with remorse, the girl explains that someone else is the father, but he dodged so she accused the monk because she knew he would help her. The people come to him apologizing, and taking the baby back, say, "How could we have ever believed such horrible things about you?"

The Monk replies calmly, "Is that so?"

PBS calls you the "kingpin" of the election integrity movement, which some people claim is insurrectionist by nature, a threat to democracy.

A claim which no one will explain to me.

We'd love to understand how you came to be involved in these election matters. And as you know, one question that is asked is, "Where is the evidence?"

"Where is the evidence?" That's funny. When I hear it, I want to say, "They keep it in the same closet they kept Hunter Biden's laptop and Joe's $10 million Burisma bribe."

Since November 4, 2020, a mountain of evidence has been all around us. 75 percent of the public sees it, and whether they can articulate it, they sense it. But 25 percent of the public is so brainwashed they cannot see it.

I will show you what I mean by answering your other question first: how did I get from ejecting from my company, going public about my role in the Russian Hoax, and dipping out to Indonesia... How did I get from there to the middle of this? Let me answer that first.

Go ahead. How did you get in the middle of this election scandal?

I came back from Indonesia because I received instructions to do so. I was in a far out-of-the-way island, sleeping in a hut at an obscure surf camp. I had ditched my electronics and taken a couple ferry rides and buses to get to that camp. But occasionally I returned to retrieve my electronics long enough to check in and had been receiving demands that I return to the USA. I kept ignoring them. One day I checked and got a message that said, *It doesn't matter that you're in* _____ (and named the hamlet I was in), *we can kill you wherever you are.*

I was still hesitant and replied that I thought I would be arrested or killed if I returned. I said that I would not come back until a federal I knew sent me a thumb's up.

Days later, I received photos of federal people I recognized giving a thumb's up. One of them was William Barr, sitting at his desk at the DOJ with the Washington Monument framed in the window behind him, one hand holding up a Washington Post to show what day it was, the other hand giving a thumb's up.

Attorney General William Barr.

Correct. So, I came back. Early 2020, or maybe late 2019. I was directed to support a counter-trafficking activity that was spinning up. Covid hit and all went to ground for a few months. Meanwhile, I had a tumor growing on my spinal cord that eventually reached the point that one leg went completely paralyzed. I could not walk. That took microsurgery and a month of recovery.

By August 2020 I was back in action. There was an anti-human-trafficking activity going on. Some of the people involved were cyber guys, "dolphin-speakers" as I call them, who are useful when disrupting human-trafficking networks. Some of those dolphin-speakers were making a hobby out of studying election fraud.

This was August 2020. As a pastime, they made a hobby out of teaching me about the industry of election equipment, including walking me through vulnerabilities in the architecture, hardware, and software of machines in use. They started by steering me to an HBO documentary called "Kill Chain" that is now *samizdat* [Byrne uses the Soviet term for 'banned writing & art']. And then, some YouTube videos showing how easy the machines were to hack, videos since also removed as "misinformation."

More importantly, they downloaded technical manuals, operating manuals, and sales brochures from the firms themselves. I was given chance to spend some hours with them.

There was a technical description of a three-layered database lacking "referential integrity" among its layers. (I had never heard of a database lacking referential integrity and having one could only serve one purpose that I could think of, like a corporation keeping three sets of books.) The operating manuals spoke to issues like "mass adjudication" with none of the references to integrity one would expect. The sales literature even seemed to give a nudge-and-a-wink regarding the "flexibility" it gave election administrators.

There was also a study done by California's Secretary of State in 2007, a woman. She formed a commission of computer scientists from UC Berkeley, Stanford, JPL, etc. to study these systems. They concluded the technology was garbage. Junk-ola. It violated basic tenets of computer security. In one spot in the report, they went so far as to suggest that the systems were so porous from a security point of view they may have been *designed* to be vulnerable.

Around that same year, the European Union looked into these systems. As I recall, they reported, and forced admission that, when one pierces all the M&A and licensing agreements, the operating system in these machines is actually *owned* by entities in Venezuela.

They clued me in on election scandals occurring globally. Philippines in 2010 and 2016, Ukraine 2014, Iraq 2008, Ghana, Kenya, and other African states. In each, ballot-counting was interrupted, then when counting resumed, there appeared a trademark artifact:

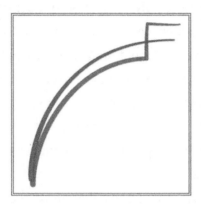

In June 2022, the DHS issued a report[6] that could have been titled, "Patrick Byrne Was Right Again. Again." They listed nine major security lapses in one brand of machines.

Read that report. It represents my state of knowledge on about October 20, 2020.

The election came two weeks later. For the first time in US history, a city stopped counting ballots. How odd.

And it was not just one city, it was six. How *especially* odd.

And it was not just *any* six cities, it was six anchor cities for six swing states. Cities with two-thirds of their state's vote. How odd.

The Media asks, "Where's the evidence?" That *is* evidence. No one ever explained it, really. Six different cities, six *different* reasons, but

---

6. https://www.deepcapture.com/2022/06/dhs-issue-report-patrick-byrne-was-right-again-again/

what do you know? They each flip a swing state. Which flips the electoral college. Which flips the White House. And they all decide to do this first-in-America event of stopping ballot-counting on the same night.

Seem odd?

You see, there are about 3,000 counties in America. On Election Day, we really hold 3,000 separate elections. To steal the White House, one does not *need* "widespread election fraud": one needs *deep* election fraud in six counties, each of which is two-thirds of the vote of a swing state. Narrow, deep fraud in those six cities flips those six swing states, and flipping those swing states flips the electoral college, which flips the White House.

And what do you know? That set of six cities in six swing states.... are the six cities that stopped ballot-counting on November 3, 2020! How odd. You get it?

The improbability of that constellation of events is a layer of evidence at 30,000 feet.

Then we drop to 3,000 feet: statistical improbabilities in outcomes. The kinds of things Seth Keshel finds. 18 of 19 "bell-whether counties" voting for Trump, yet Biden wins. Things like that. Did you know that in 2020 more Black people voted for Biden than had voted for Obama in either of his elections? I always knew Black folk *liked* Barack Obama, but it turns out they are just *wild* for Joe Biden.... But only in Philadelphia and a handful of cities. Does that sound plausible?

Perhaps you mean, patterns one can spot from 300 feet, so to speak: "Where is evidence of systemic misconduct in the election?" To see this requires understanding what went on in each state beyond what was reported in the newspapers. Think of this as the view from one hundred feet.

Within a day or two of the election, I was in Washington, DC, setting up rooms with researchers and dolphin-speakers. I knew that, at the end of the day, whatever legal process came along, the lawyers could do no more than write each other memos until there were dolphin-speakers and researchers surfacing data.

Because I was first to go on TV and say that Election 2020 was rigged, soon citizens groups were sending delegations to find me in DC. Who were they? It turned out that in many states, so many people experienced irregularities that citizens quickly found each other and swirled grassroots groups into existence, selecting leaders who assembled teams in their own states to start gathering affidavits and other evidence. Then they were flying "ambassadors" to DC to find me. I put them up in hotel rooms scattered around DC and set up debriefing teams with retired military and law enforcement. With all that information flowing in from witnesses across many states at once, the patterns in the misconduct of Election 2020 became evident, and those patterns precisely fit the methods of rigging elections about which I had been learning for the two months preceding the election.

So perhaps you meant, "Where is the *forensic* evidence?" The view from three feet, so to speak. Well, re-counting pieces of paper gets nowhere. To find out if each ballot came from a real voter requires examination of the *systems*. Regarding that, the same people who ask, "Where is the evidence?" are the people who since November 4, 2020, have fought teeth-toes-and-fingernails to make it impossible to examine those systems.

Remember, all we wanted to do is examine hard drives from six places where ballot-counting paused for hours. Each for a different reason. The investigation could be done in days. This battle ripping our country apart could be solved with a week's work. But for three years, five of those six counties have blocked having their drives inspected. *That's* evidence. To a guy who solves problems and not merely opines from lofty heights, their opposition to inspection of hard drives is evidence. I hear cockamamie claims that inspecting those hard drives would be a threat to democracy, or a crime against humanity, but no one explains why.

The sixth city, Phoenix, Arizona, which is to say, Maricopa County… The Arizona Senate issued a subpoena for their hard drive, along with lots of other things. Maricopa County fought the subpoena for six months. *That* is evidence.

Then when a court *ordered* them to turn it over and they could no longer stall, the night before they turned it over, they erased the election database. *That behavior is also evidence.*

Six months later, when they were challenged for having erased the data, they said that they had not *actually* erased it, they had *duplicated* it then deleted it…but when asked for the duplicate, they refused to turn that over. *That is evidence.*

And incidentally, the subpoena had requested their duplicates as well, so their ruse was legally meaningless. They doubly defied a subpoena. *That is further evidence.*

Such behavior would normally be decisive in the court of public opinion.

In any case, I get ahead of myself. There in November 2020, we had quickly organized so that information from voters around the country was funneled into affidavits pouring into Washington, DC. We did, intending to provide it to whatever lawyers or government agents appeared, wanting to get to the bottom of things. Rudy and Sidney and others showed up wanting it. But trying to work with that legal layer between us and the White House was (as a Master Chief we met at the time said) like watching a half-dozen monkeys try to fuck a football. At first, I thought I'd never seen anything like it, but in time I realized that I had seen things just like it before: any time I've seen a group of lawyers try to manage a project.

As an entrepreneur, watching lawyers organizing under stress was unbearable. Given that I knew we were undergoing a psyop to end the USA, it was a nightmare. Unlike General Flynn, the President's people clearly saw me as some rich guy on the side who was writing checks, and had no sense how to work with me to create a fluid, agile, task-oriented enterprise. We had stunning assets, information was flowing up from states, the White House was scrambling for help, but it was gunked-up by lawyers with their own priorities, which included endless agenda-less bull-sessions discussing past triumphs, internal jockeying for court favor, podcasts, positioning things so they could take credit, and so on and so forth.

I saw days ticking by and this disorganized shitshow going off half-cocked over and over. Rudy's press conferences about Joe Frazier still voting, Sidney filing briefs that I doubt she even read, filled with typographical errors. Trump told half-truths by mediocre intermediaries.

What was your famous December 18 Oval Office meeting really about, and is it true you snuck into the Oval Office?

True-ish.

The first thing to know is that in 2015, President Obama signed an executive order which said: If a foreign entity interferes in an election, the president has a range of powers, from running an investigation, to a Presidential Commission, to re-running that election. And in 2018, Trump renewed Obama's EO or signed a similar EO.

The second thing to know is that in late 2020, USG itself made a number of statements:

- October 9, DHS published its "Threats to the Homeland" annual report, identifying elections as a primary target of foreign powers.

- October 21–22, DHS and FBI made joint public statements: *Our election systems are currently under attack by Iran and other hostile nations.*

- On November 3, they updated that statement: *Iran has successfully hacked one state's election systems, are going after others, and other hostile powers have joined in the attack on these other states.*

- On December 6, the DHS & FBI put out a statement that an unprecedented, massive cyberattack was occurring against the USA.

- December 13, DNI-DSH announced the USA had been hacked... straight through to the teats. 425 of Fortune 500 firms and CIA-DOD-NSA-DHS-CISA-State etc. All hacked because they used "SolarWinds Orion".

Our view was once that December 13 statement from the DNI appeared, there were more than enough statements from the USG *itself* that the Executive Orders signed by Obama and Trump were tripped. Our argument had precisely 0 to do with theories of vote-flipping from space, or South Korean jets flying in ballots, or any of these claims that mainstream media parade as being ridiculous. That was all beside the point. The statements of the federal government itself tripped the relevant Executive Orders. Once the December 13 SolarWinds statement came out, Mike, Sidney, and I all saw that and wanted to make that case.

It is difficult getting to see a President. Finally, around 6:00 p.m. on Friday, December 18, I called a couple staffers whom I had gotten to know, reminded them that since I met them six weeks earlier, they had been inviting me for a White House tour, and told them I wanted to take them up on their offer *right now*. Somewhat confused, they agreed to meet me by the White House gate in thirty minutes. I went up and told General Flynn and Ms. Powell that we had an appointment at the White House, perhaps leaving them with an impression it was with someone other than two staffers. Only when we got over to the White House and inside the gates of the White House, and all parties met up, did the situation become clear to everyone.

In any case, from there we improvised around the Eisenhower building into the West Wing until we got down the hall from the Oval Office. President Trump walked by the open door of the Oval Office, still dressed in blue tie and uncreased suit and at 7:30 p.m. He saw me down the hall in a motorcycle jacket, Lululemon shirt, and jeans, and looked startled. Then Mike and Sidney stepped around the corner as well, and the President waved us all in.

I think that counts as, "Yes." In any case, what happened when you met?

We were asked to step aside while the President asked a woman, it may have been the famous "Cassady," to set up some chairs in the Oval Office. Three were in a crescent in front of the Resolute Desk, one positioned behind those three in a position I'll call "Right Field." I took Right Field while the young female, then Mike, then Sidney fanned out on the bases in front of me.

For a couple minutes there were pleasantries. Trump greeted Sidney distantly but professionally. He then faced Mike and asked him how he had been since he got the pardon, asked after his wife. He turned and acknowledged the young female attorney, and she explained briefly how she fit into things.

Then he turned to me and said, "Hello, Pat. You know, during the campaign you said some pretty unkind things about me."

I told him the truth: "Yes, Sir, I did. I had also just said a lot of awful things about Hillary, and I had to balance it out. Some of the thing I said about you I meant; some I did not mean. My feelings towards you have warmed since you became president. But none of that has anything to do with why I am here. I'm here because this election was rigged."

President Trump replied (and I only include this from a desire to be historically accurate), "You know Pat, in certain circles people speak very highly of you. You have a wonderful reputation, among certain people."

I said, "Thank you" and nodded.

Trump then turned back towards Mike and Sidney and indicated for them to explain what we were doing there. That was the last I spoke for perhaps twenty–thirty minutes.

Sidney took the lead on familiarizing President Trump with the two Executive Orders I have explained. As each was presented, Trump stopped our talking, studied the EO in question for perhaps forty-five seconds, then continued the meeting showing full understanding. He's a quick study, I am saying. I had not expected that.

General Flynn and Sidney Powell together presented the then-recent statements from the federal government. We did not have the

October 9 DHS annual report printed, but we had a folder with each of the other federal announcements in it. Again, Trump took each in turn and scanned it, then asked General Flynn about it, who answered with occasional input from Sidney. Zero percent, and I mean zero percent, of what was presented had anything to do with stuff you have heard about: South Korean jets flying in ballots and such. It was all straight out of government statements. And reviewing a couple executive orders.

Finally President Trump picked up the last document, an action plan of several pages we were asking him to sign. Out of the range of options the Obama/Trump EOs gave, we were recommending the lightest footprint option: a quickie investigation to be conducted in two weeks by the DHS. That was the only document that President Trump did not read, but just rifled through, then looked up confused and said, "So what are you asking me to do?"

I spoke up at last. "Put us in, Coach. Put *us* in. We'll get to the bottom of this."

Trump indicated for me to continue.

I told him that if he accepted our claim that *these* Executive Orders were triggered by *those* federal statements, we wanted him to order an investigation. If he did so, there would three decisions to make, each with a spectrum of options from light-footprint to heavy-handed.

I paused to give President Trump time to process, which he did, then nodded to continue.

"The first question is, '*Where* is to be investigated?' There, Sir, your choices are six, thirteen, or thirty-one counties. The obvious six where interruptions occurred. But there are thirteen that look suspect. And we have also selected a total of thirty-one, a mix of rural, urban, and suburb, Democrat, Republican, White, Black, Hispanic, that will let us answer that question political scientists have wondered about forever: how much fraud is there in US elections?"

Trump immediately beckoned towards the low end of the spectrum I had laid out with my hands, saying, "No no, go with six."

"The second question is, '*What* is to be investigated?' We could have ballots inspected on livestream TV. We could *image* hard drives in the machines in those six counties then take those images to government facilities for inspection. We could *remove* hard drives and take them back to a government facility for inspection. Or we can *remove entire systems* and take them back to government facilities for inspection. The last would be most complete, but the truth is, Sir, if we just image the hard-drives it is about 80 percent as good as everything else, and far less intrusive."

President Trump asked me to repeat this, which I did. He again beckoned towards the light end of the spectrum I had laid out with my hands, indicating the image-the-hard-drives option. "Just do that then," he said.

"The third question is, 'Who is to do it?' Sir, it could be the DHS or the FBI." (In the document we gave Trump it was written "DHS," but I went off-script.) "Please consider the possibility that what we are experiencing is a breakdown in trust in a core institution of society. I am not sure the FBI and DHS are trusted these days. I know that there is a taboo against involving the military in elections, but please consider the possibility of bolting Federal Marshalls to National Guard cyber teams. I understand that there are strong cyber-capabilities in the National Guard. The judiciary and military are the most trusted institutions in our society: the US Marshalls work for the Courts and the National Guard are our 'citizen soldiers.' Using them would be the quickest way to re-inject trust into the situation."

To his minor credit the President's lawyer, Pat Cippolini, waited until I finished, then rose and spoke for the first time. He said something like, *Mr. President, the public will go nuts if they see a single uniform anywhere near this.* He made a thirty-second argument.

The president turned to Rudy and Mark Meadows, who had been on the speakerphone throughout. They each took twenty seconds to echo those thoughts.

The President turned to General Flynn to ask his opinion. Mike was thoughtful for a moment, then said, "The DHS has units that are perfectly adequate for this."

Trump turned back to me and said, "OK, DHS."

I broke protocol (I learned later) by re-pitching my case. I said, "Sir, it is your call of course, but..." then asked him to reconsider the collapse in trust, individual US Marshalls bolted to small National Guard cyberteams—"

With a wave of his hand Trump cut me off: "No uniforms, Pat."

So three decisions were made by Trump, each with the lightest footprint possible.

At that point I said, "Mr. President, that document in your hand says we can have this done in two weeks. Tonight is December 18: if you sign it, we can have an answer for the nation by New Year's Eve. But the truth is, we think we will have an answer in a week, Christmas Eve. And the *truth* is, I think we will be able to tell you in a few days if we are finding what we expect to find. And Sir, if we do not, I think you are going to have to concede immediately—"

President Trump cut me off to say, "Pat, you have *no idea* how easy that is going to be. I will have *no problem* doing that. On January 20, Marine One is going to land right over there *[he turned at the Resolute*

Desk and pointed to his right out the window to the South Lawn of the White House]. I can walk out of here and fly away knowing I accomplished more in four years than has ever been done. I will *never* spend another day in this city again. I've got my golf courses, I've got my friends… believe me, Pat, my life is going to get a *lot* better. But if I think this election has been stolen, and there are foreign nations involved… can I really do that? How can I do that?"

The only mention of January 6 that evening was *me*, pointing out, "Sir, you don't have to sign this tonight. You may want to study and think. But you cannot wait much past New Year's to sign it, because it will take us at least a few days to execute. In any case, please know I think you cannot wait until January 6 and, if things do not go your way, ask us to do it then. That would be 'sore-loserism.'"

Trump nodded in agreement.

There was also a moment when the President and I were half-alone, moving through a doorway together. Trump leaned in close to me for emphasis: "Pat, I mean it, you have *no idea* how easy it is going to be for me to get on that helicopter. I'm going to be with friends, I'm going to be golfing, I am going to be enjoying my life… I'll have *no problem* walking out to that helicopter. But how can I do it if I think this was rigged and another nation might be behind it?"

Trump was roiled by moral anguish. In my view Trump's moral reflection was entirely appropriate. Everyone knew what novel Constitutional moments we were living that evening, and everyone in the room conducted themselves like it could have been recorded and played for posterity. But Trump's moral anguish was particularly highlighted for me. He correctly believed the election had been rigged, he correctly suspected a foreign government's involvement, and he correctly worried that he would be surrendering the country if he did nothing about it.

I may even be understating things slightly: there may have been *two* times at the Resolute Desk he made that point to me plus the *one* time alone as we walked through a doorway (but in any case, he made that point to me at *least* once from the Resolute Desk and once as we moved through a doorway). I emphasize this because the false narrative has been that he was a tyrant clutching at power. Just the opposite was true: it was clear he personally was longing to be done with Washington. But he was torn from a sense of duty, and was confused, as were so many.

What happened after the Oval Office?

Well, I have recounted the substance. We broke for thirty minutes with the idea of reconvening upstairs in the "Yellow Oval" of the residence. During that half hour, Rudy Giuliani came in from his dinner and met in the Cabinet Room with Sidney, Mike, and me. Then we all went to the Yellow Oval and much of the meeting was repeated for two more hours. Then we left at about 12:15 a.m.

It turns out that as soon as we left, Rudy Giuliani turned Trump around within two minutes by telling him, "We will all end up in prison if you go ahead with Byrne's plan."

If that is what that happened, why didn't others tell that to the J6 Committee? Why did anyone take the Fifth?

The way it works is, once you go under oath, if they ask you "How do you like the weather?" and you answer, then when they ask you legal questions looking to nail you and you try to take the Fifth, they say, "You already answered *some* questions, you cannot pick and choose." I may be exaggerating, but not by much. Others had legal privileges to maintain. Some have had enough DOJ trauma to want to avoid more.

And you?

Not me. I'm in my prime.

You know, I spent $50k taking out ads around Washington telling the J6 Committee to have me in. I'd come in under oath, no lawyer, and answer all their questions. They dodged me for nine months before finally having me in. I told them all that I have told you. I heard later that the lead investigator, a Mr. Marc Harris, decent-seeming fellow, tells people that the J6 investigation fizzled because "Patrick Byrne covered for Trump." The reality is I did not "cover for Trump"; I told the precise truth. But the truth puts a hatchet in the head of the fake narrative they were trying to create.

What was the narrative you think they were trying to create?

That there had been a Color Revolution planned, we were there to brief it to Trump, and J6 was an outgrowth of that. That's 100 percent fabrication. As was the "military seizing voting machines across the nation." The written plan was DHS cyber teams, and the discussion settled on *imaging* hard-drives in *six* counties for later analysis. The only mention of "military" was *me* proposing that instead of using DHS we use Federal Marshalls stapled to National Guard cyber teams, which was immediately rejected by everyone in the room including General Flynn and shot down twice by Trump. The only mention of J6 was *also* me, in the context that President Trump should not wait until J6 then activate our investigation.

What can they charge Trump with? He saw me outside his office, beckoned me in, listened for four hours, and decided against me.

What can they charge anyone else with? I am the one who *yenta'd* the meeting together. I was the one who briefed the options.

So charge me first. I conned my way into making the meeting happen, and I was the one who laid out the options. So if the fact of the meeting or its substance were seditious, I am the primary person they should charge.

Three hundred million Americans signed a letter asking me to stop the "systemic corruption infiltrating our federal government." I'll meet the DOJ in any court in the land and defend my actions. Plus, I had my mental GoPro running, and think history should know the truth about what went down.

Incidentally, my code name in parts of the government is "Parrot" because I have what is called an "eidetic memory." That is because of my ability to focus intently on something and remember it. I can sit in a meeting for hours, focus, walk out then write a twenty- to thirty-page reconstruction that is more or less verbatim. They have never had me wear a wire on anyone because I can do that. The story I have told you here is precisely accurate.

Didn't Maricopa's audit show Biden won?

That is the biggest lie I have ever seen the press sell the gullible. First, in any normal world, once Maricopa deleted their hard drive they failed the audit. "Failed: Deletion of Records" it is called. The auditors could have stopped there because after that there was no way to audit the election. Not really. They could hold sheets of paper up to lights and such, but there was no way to unscramble which ballots were legit and which not. Setting that aside, what they found was that while Biden "won" by 10,800 votes, the ballots did not reconcile:

- 255,326 early votes had no provenance (but simply "appeared");

- 57,734 ballots had illegal sourcing (e.g., they were mailed to someone who moved out of state years ago but voted anyway);

- >17,000 ballots were photocopies (i.e., unambiguously illegal);

- One day before complying with the subpoena, Maricopa deleted > 1 million election files (each file is one federal and one state felony);

- 15 other felonies occurred whose effect on ballots is impossible to quantify.

So if we turn a blind eye to 600,000 ballots violating Arizona and federal law, then yes Biden wins by 10,800 votes.

In addition, the recent Kari Lake trial exposed that in the 2020 election, Maricopa received 1.2 million mail-in ballots and accepted every single one. Maricopa certified that they examined 1.2 million signatures on 1.2 million ballots, and they were all good.

How do we estimate what 1.2 million ballots without rejections mean for an election? How many would they *normally* reject? Does the fact none were rejected mean Maricopa neglected to verify signatures? If so, did *others* know that was their intent and take advantage of it? How much did *that* effect the vote? There's no way of knowing. And now they have acknowledged they did not check signatures on half a million of those ballot envelopes. Which is illegal, incidentally. But again, it raises the question of: who knew that Maricopa was going to fail to perform those duties, and did they take advantage of it?

The egg can't be unscrambled.

It is a sign of either how idiotic or corrupt the media is that in the face of all that, they ask, "But where's the evidence?" Or say, "See, Biden still won by 10,800!" An honest representation would be that the audit showed there were 600,000 dubious ballots, and 1.2 million mail-ins without a rejection, but if we count them all, Biden wins by 10,800.

All over the nation, citizens have learned that trying to inspect election equipment or processes makes one suspect, or a Domestic Terrorist, and can get one indicted. In Grand Junction, Colorado, the Mesa county recorder, Tina Peters, was an apolitical grandmother who ran for office because she was concerned about waiting times at the DMV. A citizen just trying to contribute. In May 2021 Tina got wind that goons from state were coming to wipe out election data that, as Country Recorder, it was her duty to maintain. Under federal law, materials from elections have to be preserved for twenty-two months. Everything: every hard drive, thumb drive, email, every scrap of paper they ticked-and-tied on. Every file or document erased is its own federal felony. Yet goons from state were coming to erase the election files of this Colorado town.

Unbeknownst to the goons from state, County Recorder Tina Peters caused a court-certified forensic cyber guy to come make an image of her county's hard drive just *before* the goons arrived, and then again just *after* they left. So that if the goons erased what was on the hard drive, the before-and-after images of the hard drive would reveal their law-breaking.

Afterwards the two images were compared by two experts, the CEO of a cybersecurity firm and a Professor Emeritus of Computer Science from Texas A&M. Their report was called, "Mesa County Forensic Report #3."

They discovered two things on the image of the Mesa hard drive:

- The town's 2020 election had indeed been altered. After a quarter of the 100,000 votes had been tallied, a cloaked script woke up, created a new (illegal) database, siphoned over 24,000 ballots but 30,000 showed up, and the provenance of 6,000 is unclear.

- A massive cram-down of 100,000 files by the Goons from State, which is 100,000 federal felonies and 100,000 state felonies.

Remember those old photos of Black folk in Mississippi trying to vote, and facing Sheriff's deputies with German Shepherds keeping them away? How horrible a period of America history, that some citizens were so dehumanized? When election fraud happens because they inject 6,000 fake votes, there are 6,000 actual citizens whose votes are canceled, correct? So it is like 6,000 people being held at bay with German Shepherds from the voting booth. This disenfranchisement is just as horrible. It is simply done differently.

You know who is being charged with a crime? Tina Peters, the grandmother who ran for office because she wanted to reduce wait times at her DMV, and as County Recorder had the job of keeping her records safe. Even though she had that duty, and even though the black-letter law specifies that she had the power to backup, they are trying to put her in prison for twenty-five years. One felony on the grounds she gave a badge to a non-county person (my court-certified cyber-forensic friend), another for letting him into the computer center, one for lying so people she suspected of corruption would not know that she was imaging their hard drive in order to catch them if they feloniously smashed-down the data (which they did).

It's Kafkaesque. But it's a warning to those who might take a stand against corruption.

[Byrne rubs the fresh scar on his neck.]

So out of one side of their mouth they say, "Where's the evidence?" while from the other, "No one is allowed to examine any evidence!"

In reality, what has been has revealed is so much slop, so much infidelity to law, bureaucrats not bothering to follow the law, they don't even bother trying to *appear* like they follow the law anymore. Look at Maricopa's 2022 election. On Election Day, 60 percent of machines failed. Expert witnesses found the failures were programmed into those machines. Of those bad machines, 93 percent were in Republican voting precincts. As George Carlin once said, "You don't have to be Fellini to figure that out."

There is evidence in the machines' manuals, there is evidence in the ballot-counting stoppages, there is mathematical evidence, there is evidence found in the way elections were conducted, and there is the forensic evidence anywhere people have had a chance to inspect. In addition, there is behavioral evidence found in contemplating how the establishment has broken all known rules in covering this up. Unless you live under a rock, you see the evidence.

I promise, I am as correct about our election systems as I was about Wall Street settlement fifteen years ago. Someday that will be understood.

Why couldn't the government find the evidence in late 2020?

I will tell you what I know: Administrations are structured so that the White House has an ambassador to each of the departments and agencies of government. The liaison from Trump to DOJ at that moment was a seasoned woman, known in DC a serious person. The morning after the election, November 4, she went over to DOJ and confronted Barr, asking the question on the minds of hundreds of millions of Americans.

The day after the shit-show that was Election Day 2020, an election that included six big swing-state cities stopping ballot-counting, she asked, "What are you going to do about this, Bill?"

Barr told her, "The DOJ is not getting involved."

Once the grassroots folks had found me, their information was coming at me, and it had some semblance of structure, I called Barr's office and let them know I wanted to come talk to someone about what we were accumulating. I received only a message: if you have information of election malfeasance in any state, contact the US Attorney of that state.

So I tried contacting three US Attorneys: not one returned the call. Bill McSwain was US Attorney for Pennsylvania at the time. He has come out and said William Barr sent stand-down orders on conducting any investigation into Election 2020.

Recently Judicial Watch revealed that they FOIA'ed the notes and records from all DOJ/FBI investigations into Election 2020. The response came back: *After a thorough search, there are no notes or records of any interviews or investigations. None.*

That's odd, because at that time Barr claimed they conducted "dozens of investigations and hundreds of interviews and found no evidence of widespread election fraud."

You know what is also odd? The fact that Barr even *said* there was no "widespread election fraud." Barr is smart: he knows there does not have to be "widespread election fraud." There need only be fraud that is narrow and deep, primarily in six counties. It is a strawman claim. The fact Barr would even utter such a sentence tells me he was not interested in truth; he was interested in obfuscation.

Why do you think William Barr did that?

I will tell you what I know.

Someone was going back-and-forth between us with messages and information. In June of 2020, William Barr sent a message to me that ended, *If such-and-such doesn't happen, Byrne, then you and I will be meeting each other in a FEMA camp by the summer of 2021.*

William Barr sent you that message in June 2020?

Indeed he did. But then our intermediary made a visit to me on the last day of July, and during other conversations he told me that in a week Barr was going up to New York to see Rupert Murdoch and they were going to spend an afternoon alone together.

The next day, that intermediary was killed in a cross-country plane crash with an instructor on-board, flying to see someone who works with me. That seemed suspicious.

A week later somebody who survived the crash got out of the hospital and an hour later sat for an interview with me. His story: the instructor climbed the normally-aspirated twin-engine plane through an 8,000-foot Montana mountain pass on a hot August day in Montana, stalled, then got into a secondary stall. I'm a 1,500-hour twin-engine pilot, and the story hangs together. Still, I understand federal suspicion about it remains, and they may be correct.

I understand this devastated General Barr. Out of respect for Barr, I will say no more.

But if a historian looks at August 2020 Fox broadcasts, that historian will see that in the middle of the month Fox got what I can only describe as a soft-off for Donald Trump. Damned by faint praise, or damned by no praise at all. Fox was still Fox, but its editorial tone altered sharply in mid-August 2020.

Then on the evening of November 3, Fox called Arizona for Biden remarkably early.

So in 2020, Barr went from fearing in June that we were living through a revolution and if we did not defeat it, he and I would be meeting in a FEMA Camp by Summer 2021. At the start of August 2020 there was an untimely death. Then a meeting with Murdoch days later, end of the first week in August. Mid-August, Fox shifts its editorial tone. And once the fake election came, Fox calls Arizona far earlier than was justified. The election's irregularities are orders of magnitude beyond anything America had ever experienced, but Barr shrugs it off to the White House, lets them know he would not lift a finger. And orders (per McSwain) all US Attorneys not to investigate irregularities, but to leave it to states. Refuses to let his office meet me and tells me to call people who won't return calls and whom McSwain says were switched off by Barr. Yet later claims they did "dozens of investigations and hundreds of interviews," while FOIA shows they did *zero* investigations and *zero* interviews. And Barr says they found "no widespread election fraud," which is a strawman claim and suggests he looked, which is a lie (as FOIA revealed).

Connect those dots as you see fit.

But there is another angle to the Barr's DOJ of which you should know. From early 2020, DOJ was sending me messages along these lines: *Please do not go forward with any more information about what happened. Durham is ready to act, and you are going to see us round up a giant network.... You cannot believe how many we are going to arrest. We will arrest over one hundred of the Deep State by May 2020... if you can just stay silent.*

Then in May 2020 I was told it again not to go public with my story, that the Durham Report would be coming out in the Summer 2020, and I would see about 150 people rounded up. Then I was told it would be the end of summer, late September. Finally in late September, Barr came out publicly and said, "No Durham Report before the election!"

I stewed on it for a week, and then on Friday, October 2, 2020, I decided to let the DOJ know that I had no choice but to go public myself. I left a message with the head of the National Security Division, whose office is about thirty feet from Barr's: *I don't know if it is right or wrong for you DOJ folks to be sitting on all this information through the election, but I know it is wrong for me to stay silent any longer. I am sorry, but I will be going public on Monday* [October 5, 2020], *and I am giving you a few days as warning.*

Three days later, that Monday, stations from Fox to CNN and everything in between, media outlets who had been begging me to come on and share my story, suddenly all went dark. At Fox, there were three anchors begging me to come on their shows on Monday and share my whole story. But on Monday morning, they and every other journalist I knew, dozens of whom I had worked with over the years... every single one of them went dark.

Months later I was told that within the DOJ there is what one could metaphorically describe as a "button," and when they hit it on someone, the news media blanks that person out. William Barr's DOJ hit that on me on the morning of Monday, October 5, 2020, so that I could not get my story out. Journalists whom I had known for years, who took me to lunches and dinners, journalists with whom I was so familiar they'd had me meet their wives and family members, suddenly all let me know they simply were not even allowed to talk to me anymore, let alone interview me.

Now let me move on from the election to something more urgent. Are you ready?

You have stories that top that?

In 2021, it was made known to me that there were still agents looking out for me. Over time it was gradually revealed to me that there was an inter-agency team of some sort, spread across a dozen agencies, that had become the hot ticket within the three-letter agencies. It was a group of super-agents, I was told, O-5 and O-6 level, running an inter-agency group dedicated to reverse engineering the international corruption attacking the USA. I came to think of them as a "League of Shadows" who were looking out for me.

In September 2021, the Iranians reached out asking to see me. This is why I told you as much about our relationship as I did earlier. In September 2021 Iran contacted me again and let me know a big war was coming, and their call to me had something to do with peace.

I stalled them and got word to the League of Shadows, letting them know I was reluctant to get involved but would do as directed. Only then did they reveal themselves to me in person. They studied it for some weeks, then instructed me to accept the offer to meet. I specifically confirmed, "You have checked with X, you have checked with Y?" They confirmed they had checked with everyone, and it had been signed off on across-the-board.

So in November 2021, I went back to the Middle East. I met with a group including an old and special Iranian figure, who let me know a World War was coming and had a proposal to avert it. I told them I would relay the proposal, but I did not think it would fly.

While there, and through a mechanism I am not going to explain, I became aware that Hunter Biden was reaching out backchannel to the Iranian government with this offer: *You Iranians have $8 billion frozen in a bank account in South Korea. My father will unfreeze it in return* *for $800 million being funneled into a numbered account for us. And if you do this with us, it will lubricate other negotiations which have recently started between us.* By that, the Iranians believed that Hunter was referring to the nuclear negotiations which had restarted in Geneva a month or two previously. In other words, something along the lines of "Pay us $100 million and we let you keep ten nukes, $200 million for 20 nukes," etc. (but I am making up the pricing). Hunter was doing this through a middleman, the son of the Minister of Defense of Pakistan. That son was meeting with Hunter, who was then being reckless enough to leave voicemails in Iran about it. Someone in intelligence circles had acquired the voicemails.

When I returned stateside, the agencies went to work over the weekend. I was told a week later that they had confirmed it all. The voice was voice-matched to the son of the Minister of Defense of Pakistan, who had a connection to Hunter Biden. Anyway, in December 2021, I was told that the scheme was confirmed across the agencies.

Patrick, you are claiming in autumn 2021 the Bidens were seeking a bribe from Iran in return for releasing funds frozen in South Korea and going easy in nuclear talks, and the United States has been aware of this since December 2021?

That is 100 percent correct.

Now let me move on to the second event of four.

There are hacker activists around the country. They use their cyber skills to further some cause. Sometimes they are called, "hacktivists".

One group of hacktivists is called "Blue Anon": like Q'anon but Democrat. They are transsexual Democrat Party hacker activists. For example, they helped the J6 committee do facial recognition of the J6 protesters. But believe it or not, within those transsexual Democratic

Party hacker activists there is a subset who are *patriotic* transsexual Democratic Party hacker activists. And they started dealing with someone in the Dark Web who they understood could get material into the hands of the US government safely. They started funneling to that person some stuff having to do with blackmail. They did so with the understanding that it was being brought into the most incorruptible cell within the USG. It is possible they understood I was somehow involved, but I'm not certain.

I let the League of Shadows know I had no idea what was on these drives. I insisted they confirm they understood there could be absolutely anything on these drives: could be snuff films, could be nuclear secrets, could be kiddie porn. There are certain things for which there is no word in any language that excuses you for having it on your computer. Eventually I was told to retrieve and courier whatever it was. It turned out to be horrible.

[Byrne seems lost in thought for a moment.]

One piece showed that Perkins Coie had not simply directed its computer scientists in Georgia to plant information on Trump's server that would connect him to a Russian bank called "AlphaBank." In addition, the Perkins Coie computer scientists tried to plant kiddie porn on Trump. To do so they went to some Ukrainian *kiddie porn* websites and grabbed kiddie porn to inject on Trump's email server.

As I said above: there is no word in any language... yet here, Perkins Coie's computer scientists were grabbing kiddie porn on their computers to plant on Trump.

A second thing: I was given forensic information that a foreign adversary had hacked the VA Medical System. I knew the name of the country and even the individual within the VA who opened a backdoor for them. I have hesitated a long time to make that public. I did not want to be the source of any vets going off their pills. But there was a foreign intrusion, and they had access to the medical files of nine million veterans and their families.

The intrusion was focused on the imaging and pharmaceuticals systems. Theoretically they could take an image of a patient with a tumor, for example, and shift the location of the tumor on the image, so when the patient is treated with radiation the beam hits the wrong spot. That way all the blood work would be consistent with the image, but it would show up as a non-responsive tumor. Or they could fiddle with lab results or prescriptions. It is possible they were preparing to do this on specific individuals within the military they wished to kill, or it could be they were planning on doing this across nine million veterans and their families. In more normal times, I would have told the transexual hackers to penetrate further and assess, but given the state of my relationship with Uncle Sam, I thought it more prudent just to pass all the cyber-forensics regarding this to the League of Shadows for them to address.

Since the government has had this information for eighteen months, presumably the breach is now plugged. No vets should go off their medications. But in 2021 the VA Medical system was hacked by a foreign adversary.

Third, there was a breach of USG Fusion Centers in the Southeast. I saw files of what looked like 100-200 people, passports and names. I was told they were the dossiers of undercover federal agents. When I presented them to a thirty-year federal agent, he looked through and told me he recognized half a dozen of them as federals with whom he had worked. The patriotic transsexual hacktivists found it in the Deep Web, where it was for sale.

There were a couple more loads, mostly of material that fit into these categories.

In addition, dolphin-speakers communicated to me that the version of Hunter Biden's laptop that Rudy Giuliani had obtained and copied was incomplete. Hunter had BleachBit 400,000 files before turning his machine into the Delaware computer repair shop. He had selected the most damning files, deleted them, then BleachBit the hard drive.

Unbeknownst to most people, however, there is a way to recover information off a hard drive even after it has been BleachBit, if the right dolphin-speaker gets a forensic image of it.

The right dolphin-speaker got the drive. He recovered the files Hunter had BleachBit before turning his laptop into the repair shop: signature pages of contracts, porn, and texts from Hunter's phone that had been backed-up on the laptop then also been BleachBit. Those texts filled in missing pieces that Hunter had wished to conceal. I gave this forensic image of Hunter Biden's laptop with those 400,000 files recovered to the League of Shadows as well.

Somewhere in those months news broke that the FBI had "lost" Hunter Biden's laptop. That is another half- truth. They may have "lost" the physical laptop, but they have a forensic image of the hard drive, including 400,000 files he deleted with BleachBit that my dolphin-speaking-friend recovered. They have it from me.

Eventually FBI got word back to me: "Did you keep a copy of that hard drive?" I had not. But it seemed an odd question. I came to suspect that Director Wray and Attorney General Garland caused the hard drive I had sent to be destroyed. Maybe Wray stood in the room when it was nuked in the FBI lab. That would be sad, if an FBI Director destroyed evidence. That would be a dirty cop.

I realized that was going to happen to all I had couriered for them. So I sent instructions to the hacktivists, including the patriotic Blue Anon transsexual Democrat Party hacker activists, to prepare another copy of their information.

I caused the forensically complete image of Hunter Biden's laptop to reach Garrett Zeigler, one of the young men whom I had met in the White House (Garrett is in fact the fellow who let me in on December 18). As a result, he and his "Marco Polo" operation were unique among those looking into Hunter's drive in that they had our full version, the one that included the worst 400,000 files Hunter erased just before turning his laptop in.

I took 2.5 Terabytes of the other stuff I mentioned and caused copies to be stored in safe places. For when we have a functioning United States Government again.

My understanding is that the information I brought in, particularly the stuff linking Perkins Coie to kiddie porn, was (metaphorically speaking) so radioactive that the leadership of this immensely success-ful inter-agency task force—one that had operated for several years with great success, which had gotten large budget increases and was considered the hot ticket in a dozen three-letter agencies—its *leader-ship* was called in and suspended or fired. That task force's agents got reassigned around the country. Two decided, *Screw this*, and walked into Congress as whistle-blowers. Then six. Then a dozen. Then twenty. Then 100. Then more....

Remember hearing about that last summer? I have spoken to mem-bers of Congress of late who say they are so swamped with federal whistle-blowers they do not have enough staff to handle them all. I think the first snowflakes in that avalanche of federal whistleblowers were from that high-speed team dealing with me. And they brought into

Congress the stuff I have told you about here. Along with, no doubt, other stuff they had seen on their own.

We have reached the point where the United States Government is what in MMA they call "a fighter no longer intelligently defending himself." So they were doing the right thing to go to Congress. The owners of the government, We the People, need to know that our government has jumped its tracks.

And I am right to tell the public about it.

There are two last things to tell you. To understand them, you need to know that sometimes whistleblowers reach out to me. I hate mentioning that because my experience is that anytime I do, no matter how I do it, more whistleblowers reach out.

So let me be clear: *I want no more whistle-blowers ever to reach out to me ever again in my life. Please: never again.*

OK, with that said… two sets of whistle-blowers reached out to me. One came through a fancy, high-end lawyer in DC. His client worked at CIA, maybe CIA security. The lawyer delivered to me this detailed message:

In late 2014–early 2015 CIA Director John Brennan had visited the UK, and several months later had visited Moscow.

On the visit to the UK, Director Brennan had slipped his security and been seen in the back of a limousine where he rode for three hours. It was believed that the head of the UK branch of the FSB (which used to be called, "KGB") was in the limousine.

Several months later, in April 2015, Brennan went to Moscow. He slipped out of the US Embassy at 3:30 a.m. and got in the back of a limousine in which he rode for 2.5 hours. It was thought the Director of the Russian FSB was in that limo.

That is interesting on many levels. Here is one. This was never mentioned in the US from what I saw, but Maria told me she had first visited the USA in February–March of 2015, not July. She was on a delegation with the Central Bank of Russia, acting as assistant to the Vice Chairman of the Central Bank, Senator Alexander Torshin.

From the story I told earlier, I was clear since November 2015 that they were plotting a Russian Hoax. But I said I guessed that possibility in September 2015. And given when their out-of-character behavior started, in retrospect I saw that it may have been as early as *July* of 2015 that they were planning it, and that is why their responses to me were out of character.

But consider this hypothesis (and this is no more than speculation). Imagine this is what happened:

In February–March 2015, Maria Butina visits the US for the first time as part of a Russian Central Bank delegation. She gets noticed. I promise, there is no way she would not be noticed. I have not dwelled on it, but let me explain more fully.

Again, Maria Butina is an extraordinary human. Top graduate of Russia's special school for super-gifted kids. University and master's degrees in political science, knows our liberty tradition better than almost any American I know, talks fluently about Locke and Milton Friedman and Bitcoin. She did her master's at American University in Washington while all this was going on, and I saw her transcript: it was a couple dozen A+. She is also a physical specimen: champion power lifter, runner, kickboxer. Selected by a dying Mikhail Kalashnikov to lead the organization he founded. That alone should tell any but the most historically illiterate that she is indeed an extremely special young woman.

My point is, when in March 2015 Maria Butina was in Washington with the Russian Central Bank, there is *no way* she was not noticed before she flew home.

And if I got that whistleblower's information correct, it was the following month, April 2015, that Brennan went to Moscow and in the wee hours slipped into a limousine with Russian FSB.

Consider the possibility that what he said in the back of that Moscow limousine was, "Last month you had that red-headed intellectual over in DC. Send her back and we'll have some fun with her."

In May 2015, Maria gets asked by Russian Central Bank Vice Chair/ Senator Alexander Torshin to come to America for her graduate studies, try to build relationships into Camps Hillary, Cruz, Rubio, and Trump. Maria, bright-eyed idealistic graduate student of political philosophy, dreaming of playing a role bringing about world peace, agrees.

In July 2015 Maria comes over, flies directly to Las Vegas. Asks Trump a question. Then goes on to DC to live with her Republican boyfriend and schmooze around political circles, bright-eyed at the possibility of being a "'citizen diplomat'" playing a role in nudging the world towards peace. An idealist who lets people know within ten minutes of meeting them that she is connected to powerful players in Russia, not hiding her hope to be part of some thawing of relations. Having dinners and posting it on Facebook. Not knowing that from Day 1, in the background the entire thing has been instigated by, and is being observed and managed by, CIA Director John Brennan.

If this hypothesis is true, it means the Russian Hoax did not start in September 2015 or even July 2015. It started in *April* 2015.

As I said, that is only speculation. But if it happened that way, it is interesting for this reason: it was two months before Trump came down an escalator to declare his candidacy.

Which confirms it was just part of constructing the elements of a *coup* on whomever came to power, like bribing Hillary Clinton so that she could be blackmailed.

What went wrong with that plan was the day Maria landed in the USA, in Las Vegas, she heard my keynote and sought me out. And ended up sharing not just her invitation but her intentions, not knowing my relationships meant I needed to report it. Why?

- Because I held a security clearance, and was being invited to Russia;

- Because I could indeed have opened doors into think-tanks within foreign policy circles, but I first needed to get a thumbs up;

- Because I worried about her schmoozing around our political class;

- Because I wanted to witness whatever was drawn on this *tabula rasa*.

From their indecisive response, I suspected they were cooking something up. Certainly as early as September 2015, maybe as early as August 2015. And if my story about Brennan and the limousine is true, it was April 2015. *Before* Trump announced.

Meaning: The Russian Scandal was set up so that *whoever* emerged within the Republicans was going to slam into a Russian scandal. It was not about Trump at all.

Even if this hypothesis fails, I can promise, in the July–September 2015 timeframe (*not* 2016) they were definitely setting it up on Cruz, Rubio, and Trump. And anyone else who emerged on that side of the aisle.

What you know now is the truth. A Congressional Committee could verify every word of this in forty-eight hours if they wanted to. The difference between it and what you have previously been told is a measure of how corrupt our systems are. The DOJ, the Mueller commission, the Senate Intelligence report, the Durham Report, the Media. It has all been a seven-year corrupt charade.

This is a lot to take in.

I am sure. But I have one final story on corruption. It stems from the second of the two sets of whistle-blowers I said reached out to me.

Whistle-blowers from within the DOD and law enforcement communities reached out and found me for the same reason others find me. *Again, please, no whistleblowers ever call me again.* But they found me and began communicating with me about a situation.

There is a recent book called *Code Over Country: The Tragedy and Corruption of SEAL Team 6* by Mathew Cole. It claims that within the SEAL community there has been a rogue element, particularly within Team 6 since its founding under Marcinko.

How this came about was explained: there is a SEAL who went to the same Delaware high school as Biden, but who is younger, about my age, and of whom there is evidence of contact with Biden in his youth. This man was carried through BUDS (so his teammates say). He was selected for SEAL Team 6 after only three years in the SEALs and no deployments (normally, candidates for SEAL Team 6 need eight years in the teams and have at least three deployments). According to the teammates who went through SEAL Team 6 training, he was carried through that training program as well. He rose within ST6 until he commanded it, so they told me, managed its brand, and built an organization where many honest, patriotic SEALs are unwittingly shielding a small cadre of criminals. But he is a pure Alinskyite, they maintain, and developed within ST6 a strain of operator who is dirty like he is, and whom he could employ in a personal rogue mafia, buried among the honest "soft-eyed boys" of ST6.

After 9/11, laws were passed encouraging agencies to hire from SEAL Team 6 and similar Tier 1 units. Bad actors from within ST6, as well as clean ones, got sprinkled across the agencies. There the bad ones have come to act as a Praetorian Guard for the Deep State. More specifically, like a *late Roman Empire* Praetorian Guard, one that not just *guards* the emperor, but *chooses* the emperor. This Praetorian Guard has been protecting the Biden-Clinton nexus of corruption for two decades.

Not all ST6. Just an element within. And this corrupt mafia's "Queen Bee" (as he is known within) had by that time risen to a high-ranking position within the US Special Operations Command. That is what this network explained to me over a series of interactions.

I got all of this into the hands of the League of Shadows. Within a month, the man in question, who had risen nearly to the top of SOCOM, resigned his position.

Weeks later, *Code over Country* appeared. Mathew Cole must know insiders, too.

Surely most SEALs, including SEAL Team 6, are great Americans. Heroes. But there are some who are not, and they have worked themselves into every three-letter agency in government. It is a massive CI problem that needs to be studied. I will stop there.

Are we living through a revolution?

At one level, yes, "Maoism with American Characteristics," as I said. But more specifically, you are living through a Bezmenov Model Psyop.

A 'Bezmenov psyop'? Explain that.

A Bezmenov Psyop is a way of taking over a country without firing a shot. It comes in four stages: Demoralization, Disorientation, Crisis, and Normalization. The idea is to *demoralize* the target nation's population to weaken them, then get them so *disoriented* the world seems psychotic to them, then force a *crisis* down their throat and say, "The only way back to sane reality and *normalcy* is to accept what just happened."

For us, Stage 1 (demoralization) was Covid-19. The response to Covid-19 was unserious from a scientific point of view in two ways. The first way it was not based on science was the denial of early treatment, and the second way was its attachment to the "Woke-Poke" vaccine.

Covid-19 received no early treatment. Ask any doctor to name an upper respiratory virus that, when the patient presents at the hospital and tests positive, the patient is told, "Go home, rest, come back if it gets bad." They don't. Patients are given antibiotics to avoid bacterial pneumonia, anti-inflammatories, in some cases, drugs that prevent viral replication.

But Covid-19? "Go home and have some chicken soup, come back if your lips turn blue." DARPA has leaked that CDC and FDA knew in 2006 that Ivermectin, HCQ, and Zinc work on Sars-1. Covid-19 comes from Sars-2, which differs genetically by 23 percent. It could have been snuffed out with Ivermectin, Zinc, and HCQ in weeks, as some nations did.

In addition, the vaccine-mania was unconscionable. Vaccines need long-term testing, especially when they rewrite human DNA. It does not matter how many billions of people you test for a few months; you still have zero long-term results.

There is a book in computer science, *The Mythical Man-Month.* Managers hear that a software project will take four people ten months and think, "Well that is 4 X 10 = 40 man-months. So I'll just throw 20 people at it and get it done in 2 months because 20 X 2 = 40." In fact when they go from four to twenty people working on the project, they find it takes two *years*, because the coordination cost increase outweighs the horsepower increase.

Similarly, it doesn't matter how many people you test a vaccine on for three months; you still have no long-term data. You can test a *billion* people for three months, but you can't say, "We have three billion man-months of testing!" You know *zero* about long-term effects.

The response to the pandemic was unscientific both in the prevention of early treatment, and the insane emphasis on a new type of "vaccine" that is not even a vaccine; it is an mRNA-based nanotechnology that rewrites peoples' genetic codes. They needed the pandemic for social separation and anxiety.

That was Stage 1: "Demoralization."

Stage 2, "Disorientation"? That was Antifa/BLM. Taking over six city blocks of an American city and nobody doing anything about it. "Mostly peaceful protests" that injured 1,000 police and killed 33?

In October 2020 I was walking in DC near the FBI building when a bunch of leather-clad guys on motorcycles and ATVs took over the street in front of the FBI. They did donuts and wheelies for ten minutes in front of what is putatively the world's premier law enforcement organization. Unmolested. No one lifted a finger to stop them. Seem odd?

It was all to say, "This is not the America you know, it's a new world you've entered." To disorient the public.

Stage 3, "Crisis"? That's the rigged election. Enough said.

Stage 4, "Normalization"? That's Cancel Culture. They need to prohibit opposing viewpoints. That is because their ideas are bad and cannot stand on their own, and they have done evil to seize power and want no one criticizing it.

These last few years in the USA have been odd: pandemic, Antifa, crazy elections, censorship... It is a kaleidoscope to many people. If you consider the Bezmenov paradigm, you will see these four puzzle pieces fit perfectly: Demoralization (Covid-19), Disorientation (Antifa/BLM); Crisis (Election 2020); Normalization (Cancel Culture).

How about we throw some quick questions at you, for your comment?

Sounds good.

Will we ever see evidence of fraud in election 2020?

Yes. Before the next election.

If your life were a movie, what movie would it be?

It would be... a cross between *Miller's Crossing* and *Angel Heart*.

Are you afraid of being killed?

No. If they blow me up I win.

Seriously? Nothing else you feel about it?

I've died 500 times. What's 501?

What if they throw you in prison?

"Tell them to send my ass somewhere I ain't been before. Like Tahiti."

Sorry. That's something funny I heard someone say forty-seven years ago. I won't lie. I would not like it. Other the other hand, it's why I took up yoga a decade ago: I wanted something I could do in a prison cell.

Do you worry that the Senate will deny your letter, or claim that it was not intended to cover the actions you took?

Not really. Buffett has a saying about that, too. He says, "Never get in an argument about who won the 1937 World Series. It is a fact, it is a knowable fact, it is written down somewhere on a piece of paper, go look it up. Don't argue about it."

Similarly, the Senate Judiciary has confirmed to numerous people the existence of that letter. There is no reason for anyone to fight about what it says. What the letter says is written on the front of the letter. There is nothing for us to debate.

But what if the Senate Judiciary still does not back you?

I will consider that a *takeback*. And see if I ever do something like *this* for them again.

[Byrne roars at his own joke, as is his habit]

Honestly, I have been hearing for over a year that General Garland wants to indict me, but Judiciary has told him that would be a party foul. I was in ambiguous circumstances, I learned Hillary was setup only so she could be blackmailed, I had seen the Russian Hoax cooked up for a year, and they had threatened my life. Only then did I launch my rape-and-murder torpedo. I was sent to be in that position in 2006 by seven Senators who told me they needed me to disrupt the "systemic corruption infiltrating the federal institutions of our nation's government." They asked me to find them the Deep State, I found them the Deep State. And per their instructions, I didn't kill anyone. I just lured the Deep State into implicating themselves in an aggravated-rape-and-murder that never happened. Specter is laughing from his grave.

So to sum up, if I understand correctly, you claim the Deep State tricked you into setting up Hillary Clinton so they could blackmail her. And the Deep State tricked you into setting up the Russian Scandal. But you figured it out, so you boxed them in: if they wanted to continue their coup d'état, the Deep State was going to have to sign to Maria Butina being drugged and raped, and potentially murdered?

Exactly.

Were you going to kill her if they asked?

Are you insane? Of course not. I prepared two routes to get her out of the country and back to Moscow if they told me to kill her. But I knew they would not: there was no point to it. They had their own plans for her.

The point was for me to make the offer. *That* was the sting. There was no way the USG was going to let that slide. It was going to be like that torpedo-from-a-parachute we use against Russia. It would find its way to the depths of the Deep State and present someone with a dilemma.

Did it work?

In the summer of 2020 they confirmed that they had found Hillary's bribe. A government guy came from Durham to me with a photo of a statement from a bank in Azerbaijan with a numbered account holding $18 million. It had arrived in late January 2016, just as I had told them.

I could not resist asking the federal, "So how did the rape/murder gambit play?"

The federal winced and told me that the three agents had put my clues together not *minutes* after I left the room, but in *seconds*, then went back to their office and recommended scrubbing the mission. They were overruled.

"Then Patrick," he said (having trouble saying the words), "after you offered to eh-heh-heh *murder* Ms. Butina, they went back to their office and *demanded* it be scrubbed."

"But it *wasn't* scrubbed. It went on five more months," I said.

Looking up at the sky he answered, "Someone else took all responsibility."

That happened... when?

October 2016. The month Trump got in trouble for his, "grab-em-by-the-pussy" line. That same month, I put the Deep State in the position of, to continue their *coup*, they had to sign off on an aggravated rape-and-murder that never happened. Then they had me date her five more months then breakup, so that a year later, the day they needed their Russia prop, hours before Trump met Putin, they arrested Maria Butina. Ruining the Trump-Putin meeting.

They knew everything about her for three years, knew every zigzag, but arrest her the morning Trump and Putin are about to meet? That is the Deep State conducting foreign policy.

Then they kept her in a box the size of my shower stall for eighteen months. No windows. A mail slot they opened three times per day to slide a bowl of mush to her.

You remember that American college kid who did something frat-boy in North Korea? He stole a poster of Great Leader in an elevator. They sent him home three years later howling from a burlap sack, and then he died a few days later? What the Deep State did to Maria was not that bad, but close. They thought she was manipulated, seduced, drugged, raped, by a guy planning to murder her (me), as she was set up to be a hand-grenade so when the right day came, they could pull its pin, throw it into Camp Republican, then imprison Maria in a box for eighteen months feeding her mush through a mail slot. So they had someone to point to when anyone asked, "Why doesn't your Russian Collusion Drama have any actual *Russians* in it?"

Now the seduction-drugging-rape-and-murder was fabrication, but the Deep State did not know that. The prosecutorial setup was real, and eighteen months in a box eating mush through a mail slot was real. Find out who was behind that, you find who is behind it all.

What if it was Barack Obama?

I hope it is not President Obama. It would definitely hurt my feelings if it were he.

Did you vote for him?

I did not vote for President Obama, either time. I happened to like him, but I did not vote for him. Nor Trump for that matter. Journalists always write that I am a Trumplican, but I'm not. I vote libertarian, and always have. Partially because I truly am a "libertarian republican," as Milton put it, though I don't think much of the Libertarian Party. But also, because of these USG requests I never wanted to be associated with either party. For Obama and Trump, when they won, I served both with equal enthusiasm. I always considered it the honor of my life that USG tasked me to do these things, but especially when a president tasked. I was not keen on some of Obama's policies, but I liked Obama. I knew our politics overlapped but were not congruent, but of course one sets that aside. And I thought Michelle was a wonderful First Lady. I was congruent with Trump's policies, less with his style. But you know what? The way the Establishment lost its mind about him, Trump grew on me.

But as I have said, I am familiar with the ethics of military officers and how they compartmentalize their personal convictions from their sense of duty, and I always followed that same principle. Never for a second did I let the politics of the people asking me to do tasks affect my willingness to do them or how I executed them. It was only when I had arranged a fake Russian scandal, bribed Hillary to be blackmailed, then had my own life threatened, that I decided to follow Buffett's teachings, and just *fuck* them.

Why did you say it would "hurt your feelings" if Obama were behind this?

There are things I did for him that I thought would go to my grave... but here we are. Before these other matters occurred, I did things for Obama that one might consider dangerous. So I would be disappointed if the death-threat my handlers gave me originated with him.

Can you say what you did for him?

No, not really. I am not supposed to anyway. I never expected it to appear in my lifetime. But I have been put in a rather bleak situation, and I have to clean this up. I will reveal as little as possible but that lets me still make my point.

The first was the first week President Obama was in office. I was called to a government facility, briefed on a task, and told that it was at his request. I was to make my way to a country where there was no US Ambassador, contact the Chief of their Gestapo, and do a thing they needed done. I did it.

Again, why would they ask you to do that?

Because he was an old friend of mine.

President Obama was an old friend of yours?

No. The Gestapo Chief was an old friend of mine.

Why was the Gestapo Chief an old friend of yours?

We'll never get anywhere if I have to keep going backwards. The Gestapo Chief was an old friend, so I was sent to contact him and make something happen that Obama wanted done. So I did.

The second regarded a missing American overseas. My dad was dying. I was on my way to spend his last Christmas with him. I got a call. These things are never done by phone, but I got a phone call from Gregory Craig. He said he had retired as White House General Counsel a few days previously but gave me a way to verify him. I did and called him back. Craig told me there was a missing American overseas, he was running the administration's response, the computers said there was an American who was friends with a senior Al-Qaeda cleric and could deal with them safely, "...and it's you, Patrick. Is this true?"

I said, "'Friends' is a big word, but I can deal with them safely."

He told me my task, which necessitated getting in touch with various Bad Guys in a nasty part of the world, including Al-Qaeda.

I asked who was sending the order, and he gave me some government titles, but ended, "I'm looking through the trees of Lafayette Park at the White House, at the window to the living quarters of the White House, at the man who is asking you to do to do this."

So I did it. Instead of spending my Pop's last Christmas with him. He died weeks later.

You know the core media team of ISIS? The one that does the beheading videos, the pilots-burning-alive-in-cages videos? They have a photo taken on Christmas Day, 2012, in an apartment in a slum in the south of Giza, Egypt. The four of them standing arm-in-arm of a tall American guy, jean jacket, cowboy boots... That is I. That is what I was doing on Christmas Day 2012 instead of being with my Pop on his last Christmas because President Obama needed something done. Just as in early 2009 I was in another place he needed me to go. The kind of place where there was no US Ambassador.

You ask why my feelings would be hurt if the orders to frame Hillary for blackmail and to engineer the Russian Hoax were from him? Or the death threat? That's why.

So you're saying the core media team of ISIS has a selfie with you, Patrick?

They do. But to be scrupulously honest, they were Al-Qaeda when I was with them. Six weeks later they defected AQ, traveled to Raqqa, Syria, and joined ISIS, became their Media Department. But they treated me honorably.

We've confirmed that you receive such requests, but can elaborate further?

I'll tell you as best as I can figure it myself.

First, you know that old Western *Jeremiah Johnson*? There's a scene where Robert Redford finds a settler woman, her family has been butchered, she's keening by the still-warm corpses of her children.

Redford sorts things out, buries the bodies, fixes her cabin, lays in supplies, while for days she sobs and whispers to her children's spirits. As Redford leaves he tells her, "The Injuns will leave you alone now, Woman, because you are… touched."

I think I must come across as mentally handicapped, because all my life, wherever I've gone people look out for me. Even Al Qaeda and ISIS. Go figure.

Second, in 2011 or so, I was told that President Obama had given me a designation along the lines of, "National Intelligence Asset" and I was told that from that point forward, I would be used only in ace-in-the-hole situations. Again, I do not consider the work I have done ever to be "intelligence." I've never been about stealing secrets or tricking people: I just have been encouraged to keep up relationships that some might find unsavory, for the day that "certain kinds of people" want to talk.

Do you worry that the Senate will deny your letter, or claim that it was not intended to cover the actions you took?

Not really. Buffett has a saying about that one, too. He says, "Never get in an argument about who won the 1937 World Series. It is a fact, it is a knowable fact, it is written down somewhere on a piece of paper, go read it."

Similarly, the Senate Judiciary has already confirmed the existence of that letter to numerous people. So there is no reason to fight with anyone about what it says. What the letter says is written on the letter. If I am wrong, just produce the letter. But it would be ridiculous to say, "Yes there is a letter, no it does not say what Patrick says, but take our word for that." Let us not fight about who won the 1937 World Series: let's just look at the piece of paper to see what it says.

Why did you say the war in Ukraine is the most avoidable war of our lifetimes?

As a prefatory point, let me make clear that I think Putin's conduct of this war has been horrific. Nothing I am going to say should be construed to doubt that. But let me get on to a more reasoned answer.

First, I should mention that in January 2015, Vessey took me to see George Schulz and Henry Kissinger speak. Now Jack Vessey was Reagan's two-time Chairman of the Joint Chiefs. Jack Vessey often referred to himself as the founding member of "Be-Prepared-to-Nuke-Them-Until-They-Glow Club." Nobody could ever accuse him of being soft: he was a hawk's hawk. Similar things could be said of Schulz and Kissinger. Yet in 2015, all three were in full agreement that it was nuts for us to be talking about bringing Ukraine into NATO, it was nuts to be risking World War III over it. In the last two centuries Russia has been invaded five times from the West, as I recall. If we absorb Ukraine into NATO, that means we are putting American tanks 240 miles from Moscow. That is an incredibly provocative act.

There was no reason, hawks Vessey, Schulz, and Kissinger all agreed, not to take a deal where Ukraine was a neutral state, like Finland or Switzerland.

Yet since 2014 the Democratic Party and much of the Republican Party seem to have been hell-bent on provoking a war with Russia. They are a bunch of think-tank assholes who usually have never seen war, not in any meaningful sense. They may pride themselves on having flown in and out of war zones and written papers about it, but I have met many of them over time, and I promise you they are too pussified to have ever put themselves in the position of having to eat their own cooking.

Ukraine has been reduced in population from 36 million to about 21 million people in this war. About 500,000 have been killed, and another million have been grievously wounded, had legs and arms blown off, etc. The remaining millions have become refugees across Europe and elsewhere. I cannot imagine why someone would choose this outcome rather than just having Ukraine be neutral, like Finland or Switzerland.

Putin wanted a twenty-year guarantee of no discussion of absorbing Ukraine into NATO. Instead, America has a bunch of airhead politicians like Lindsey Graham competing to show how butch they are by bragging that funding Ukraine is a cheap way to kill Russians, and over chardonnay and brie at DC cocktail parties displaying their willingness to fight to the last Ukrainian. They are vile children.

Second and perhaps more importantly, in 2018 I was in Ukraine discussing business opportunities for Overstock.com. In time, the people hosting me explained that they were with one of the three dominant mafias in the Ukraine. They spent considerable time teaching me about Ukraine and what was going on beneath the surface.

After some days, they told me they had a letter for me to bring back to Trump.

I refused, telling they should just take their letter to our embassy in Kiev.

They told me, *We cannot do that, Patrick. Your embassy here in Kiev is filled with a bunch of Obama-Biden holdovers, they are highly corrupt, and they are in bed with one of our two rival mafias. Last year your country sent $5 billion to be distributed among NGOs to aid Ukraine, and $4 billion it was stolen and split up among our rival mafia, your embassy people, and the forces that control them back in America.*

It is now no longer in dispute that Hunter Biden owns 10 percent of a biologics firm called Metabiota, and that firm is a fifty-fifty partner in dozens of bioweapons labs in Ukraine whose existence had not previously been disclosed. If we were bombing Vietnam and it turned out that Richard Nixon's son owned a bunch of bioweapon labs in Vietnam, I think we would all see the logic in asking, *What the hell is* that *about?* And in insisting, *Before we drop another bomb on Vietnam, we need to know the full story on these labs and why the president's son has a major ownership stake in them.* That would be only natural, correct?

Well, the same goes for this situation, *mutatis mutandis.*

Yes, Putin's conduct of the war has been monstrous. So why instigate a war with a monster when there is an acceptable alternative? By trying to absorb Ukraine into NATO we provoked this war with no larger geopolitical objective and with a perfectly acceptable alternative ready at hand, as Vessey, Schultz, and Kissinger made clear in 2015, and which remained true right up into February 2022 when the war broke out. And given Ukraine's status as one of the most corrupt nations on the planet, and what my Ukrainian mafia friends told me about our Obama-Biden embassy in Kiev being in bed with one of the three major mafias in Ukraine, and the fact of Hunter Biden's ownership in sensitive companies in Ukraine, I think the chances are *extremely* high that the stated reasons for our war in Ukraine are smokescreen for some other real reasons, and those *real* reasons have something to do with corruption.

Does our country have any way out of the financial catastrophe we are facing?

Yes, it does. I have no idea if anyone in Washington understands it or if they could pull it off. But the template that my father and Buffett used to fix broken insurance companies is the approach that would work to rescue the US financially. That template had three steps:

1. Face your situation with candor. In the context of an insurance company, that means look at your balance sheet and recognize potholes it has accumulated in the reserves, write off bad assets, and get a look at how things *really* stand;

2. Restructure the business so it is sound on a go-forward basis;

3. On the strength of having addressed the potholes in your balance sheet and having restructured the firm so that it is sound, go recapitalize your balance sheet the play the ball where it lays.

That could be applied to the USA in a way that minimizes human suffering.

First, true up the government's corrupt accounting and see where things really stand.

Second, to make things sound going forward, switch to what Milton proposed in 1965: a Flat Tax combined with UBI (which Friedman invented, calling it a "Negative Income Tax"). The Left is pulling for UBI these days, the Right has always wanted a Flat Tax, but people forget it was Milton who proposed them, and pointed out that *if you combine them something magical happens.* I won't go into it here, but one could reduce 68,000 pages of Federal Tax Code and our Social Safety Net to two numbers: a Flat Tax Rate coupled to UBI.

Third, as far as how we "recapitalize" the USA, I will tell you about one of my favorite exchanges I ever had with Buffett. It was twenty years ago. I was bemoaning the direction of our country, pointing out it was being run like a badly managed insurance company, "...and when it collapses someday, Mr. Buffett, I suppose the rich are going to have to bail it all out?"

In an instant Buffett responded, "Well who else is *going* to bail it out Patrick, the poor? If the poor could bail it out, they wouldn't be the poor they'd be the rich." Funny.

Anyway, that is indeed the third step in the formula.

Instead, it seems we are heading down a path where the rich, the elite, have used our shoddy financial system to loot our nation dry until it's just a husk, and now they are going to kick it over and create an authoritarian Hunger Games world into which they get to escape with all the accumulated knowledge and technology of our civilization while 90 percent of people get starved off. It looks like that may be their plan, anyway.

What about you and Rudy Giuliani? You really went after him in your book.

I did not "go after him." After 9/11 I shared the same admiration for Rudy that many Americans felt. And even earlier, his work taking on

the Mob in the 1980s, made him a hero to me. Many years ago I introduced him in one of his Utah fundraisers when he ran for president.
I always admired the guy. But I had a duty to history to tell the truth
about what happened in those last two months of the Trump presidency,
so I told the truth.

In early November I went to his campaign office to brief Rudy. I
tried to talk to him about the machines used in elections and what we
were confident had happened, how it could be proven. It was a waste
of time, his office reeked of booze, it was 2:00 p.m., and he was drunk
as a skunk. He was too drunk to follow the most simplified explanation
I could muster.

His staff told me to write it up as a one-pager and bring it to Rudy
in a restaurant. I wrote and waited in my room, not getting the call to
go to the restaurant until 10:00 PM. I did and he kept me waiting for
an hour before he had someone come out and take the single piece of
paper from me to him in the back of the restaurant. I learned later that
Rudy had consumed three triple-Scotch in the previous ninety minutes.
When he got the one-pager, he tried to read it for a few seconds, then
pushed it aside and said, "I'll get to this later in the office."

Ten hours later, Rudy did that press conference with hair dye running down his face.

On the night of our December 18 White House meeting, Rudy was
at dinner with Meadows, but listened to the first part of the meeting
through the speakerphone on the Resolute Desk in Trump's Oval
Office. At 9:30 p.m. he came back into the White House, took from us
the folder of statements from the US Government that we had brought
in, sat down in the Cabinet Room, and tried to study them. He seemed
blurry, unable to focus. I watched him squint and rub his eyes and squint

some more, trying to focus and read, bleary-eyed. Still unable to focus, he pushed his glasses up on his forehead and sat flipping through them groggily for at most twenty seconds, before he gave up, pushed them aside, and just started speaking gruffly to Sidney (who was, I must say, unnecessarily prickly back with Rudy).

After their blowup, we moved up to a large living room in the Residence of the White House. The conversation there largely rehashed what had been said in the Oval Office.

When Mike Flynn and Sidney and I left the White House at 12:15 a.m., within two minutes Rudy turned Trump around, telling him, *We will all end up in prison if you go forward with Byrne's plan.*

Rudy later testified to the J6 hearing that we had given him a stack of affidavits, he had reviewed them, and decided they did not meet the evidentiary hurdle to justify going forward.

In reality, however, there was not a single affidavit in the stack. It was a stack of announcements from the federal government over the previous two months, along with the Executive Orders of Obama and Trump.

The fate of the country and arguably the world hung on the legal advice of a man so drunk he could not tell a stack of government announcements from a stack of affidavits.

Recently a sexual harassment lawsuit[7] was filed against Rudy by his assistant. You can read her description of what he is like, drunk at 9 a.m., spouting maniacal gibberish to her....

She claims that just last year, on normal workdays at 10:00 a.m., Rudy was drunk, pawing at her, and saying things like, "Come here,

---

7.https://eddsa.blob.core.usgovcloudapi.net/public/650033_2023_Noelle_Dunphy_v_Rudolph_W_Giuliani_et_al_COMPLAINT_10.pdf big tits. Come here, big tits. Your tits belong to me. Give them to me. I want to claim my tits. I want to claim my tits. I want to claim my tits. These are my tits." She has tape recordings of this stuff, of Rudy at ten in the morning, drunk as a skunk, greeting her when she arrives at work that way. On a *normal* day.

Nothing in that lawsuit is inconsistent with the Rudy I saw up close for those two months. That was the man advising President Trump as he navigated a sophisticated *coup d'état* to steal the USA. That was the man upon whom the fate of the world hung. That was the man to whom I and my dolphin-speakers were trying to explain a genius cyber-soft-*coup*.

Read that woman's lawsuit with its transcripts of recordings and decide for yourself.

Did you ever tell anyone about your relation to the US Government?

Not really. I was totally discrete for years. There were two exceptions.

At one point in 2009, my father was dying of cancer and was bed-ridden in Utah. He asked me one night why I was running around the world fighting battles with so many people. "Who elected *you* Sheriff?" he asked me. So I told him about the meeting with the seven Senators (including Orinn Hatch) and the instruction they had given me regarding how I was going to spend my life.

The next day, unbeknownst to me, my father got word to Hatch's office that he hoped the senator would come see him when next in Utah (my father and Hatch had met in DC previously). The next time Hatch was in Utah he came to the house my dad and mom were living in. He went to my Pop's bedroom and spent an hour behind closed doors with him.

Days later my father had me come over to see him. He told me that he had had Hatch over and they had spent a quiet hour alone, where my father had asked about the story I had relayed to him. Hatch had confirmed it, and talked to my father for an hour in a way that shook Pop to the core. He never told me just exactly what Hatch had said, but with a sickened expression he told me of Hatch's visit, and that he had confirmed what I had told him. Shocking me, he added, "Patrick, the senators must be in really deep shit for them to be asking you to do this…. You have to put this above everything else, even above being the CEO of Overstock." My Pop came from the Holy Church of Capital Markets, and thought a CEO had no duty other than to maximize shareholders' returns. I had never expected to hear him say anything like that.

At one point he looked up with tears in his eyes and said, "Well, at least you know what you're going to do with the rest of your life."

Whom else did you tell?

Back in 2007 I was getting death threats from Wall Street and Russia (which the FBI addressed). I went out to Hawaii looking for a way to drop out and hide if needed, looking for places and people who were off-grid. At a Poetry Slam in an Oahu dive bar I met a Kundalini Sorceress. Piercings, bindis, dreadlocks to her ankles. She spoke in gibberish, like a court jester in a Shakespeare play. The "Dread Priestess" I came to call her. She didn't ask questions about me. So from that point forward, a couple times per year, when I was most broken down, exhausted, I'd drop in and spend a week or two being vegan and do yoga, somersaults and cartwheels and light sparring (she's a black belt and a fantastic martial artist).

After I had known her six years, I decided to explain to her the nature of my relationship to the USG, the meta-tasking given me by the Senate, the Golden Letter...

She listened for about thirty seconds, cut me off, said, "Yeah yeah, I already guessed all that about you." And that was the end of it.

Other than that, no one, not even my closest friends or colleagues, knew anything about that side of my life. Until I started breaking it to several of them slowly, in 2018-2019, to prepare them for what was coming. As a prophylactic against getting killed, incidentally.

Steve Bannon seems to have enormous antagonism to you. What is that about? Your views on so many issues are carbon copies of each other. Yet he lobbies people across DC to stay away from you, and not even to talk to you.

I can simply tell you what I know.

First, yes, Bannon and I agree on most issues. So perhaps his animosity comes from what Freud called "the narcissism of tiny differences." But I think it goes deeper than that.

Second, Bannon went to the White House with Trump and lasted about six months. He began doing idiotic things, like calling himself "Trump's Brain" on the cover of *Time Magazine*. That was horrible and self-centered, ego-driven, and he deserved to be fired for it.

About a year later, I got a phone call from a journalist I know at the *New York Times*. Nathanial Popper. Nathaniel is an intelligent, hard-working journalist, and those are not things I frequently say about journalists. He wrote a book on Bitcoin called *Digital Gold*, and in that book wrote of me as a Bitcoin OG. We spoke only a few times, but he impressed me each time. Which is a rarity with journalists.

Anyway, one day probably around June 2018, Nathaniel called me from the *New York Times* and said, "What is going on between you and Steve Bannon?" I told him I had no idea what he was talking about. He continued: "Steve Bannon has been in seclusion since Trump fired him from the White House. He is beginning his reemergence into the public's eye, and as part of that he just came by and sat with the editorial board of the *New York Times* for nearly three hours. He spent the first forty-five minutes talking about you, Patrick Byrne, telling us what an incredible American you are, how you should be president someday, things like that. What do the two of you have going?"

I replied, "Nate, that shocks me. Never met the guy. Didn't know he knows my name."

"Well, Patrick, he knows everything about you and opened up his meeting with us by going on about you for forty-five minutes."

A third thing to know is that there is evidence he stabbed Roger Stone in the back. Now I know Roger, not well, we are not close. What I am about to say does not come from allegiance to Roger Stone, but out of an allegiance to the truth. Bannon said two contradictory things under oath, got away with it, and one of them is what caused Roger his legal problems.

In January 2018, Bannon told the House Intelligence Committee, under oath, that he and Roger Stone had *never* discussed Wikileaks or Julian Assange. Some months later, again under oath, Banner told the Mueller Commission that he and Roger Stone had *regularly* discussed Wikileaks and Julian Assange. The two statements were 180 degrees contradictory. Both were under oath and in front of dozens of lawyers. At least one had to be perjury.

The basis of Roger Stone's legal troubles was that second statement of Bannon's. Based on it they indicted and convicted Roger on seven counts. Trump later pardoned him.

One thing that can be said with certainty is that at least one of Bannon's statements was a lie. They could not be more contradictory, and both were under oath in front of lawyers who surely spotted the discrepancy. Yet Bannon was never charged. Nor served jail time for the crime of which he was convicted, which was not responding to a Congressional subpoena.

That constellation of facts raises the possibility that Bannon makes deals to save his own skin or is perhaps controlled opposition at times.

A fourth thing to know is that back in 2019 I did meet Steve Bannon in his DC home, "Breitbart Embassy" I think he calls it. We spent an hour together during which time he said something cryptic: he said that the real story to be told about Maria Butina asking Donald Trump that question in Vegas was how it had come to be that Trump had called on Maria in the audience. Bannon seemed to be suggesting to me that Trump's calling on Maria had not been as random as it appeared, that Maria had been pointed out to Trump and he had been *told* to call on the red-headed young Russian woman in the audience. I would not repeat something Bannon had said in private like that, but I see that Bannon has bragged of this publicly, too.

I have reviewed the videotape of Trump's 2015 appearance in Vegas, and when in the Q&A session he calls on Maria, it has the appearance of "random/not-random," if you know what I mean. If I am right about this, then whoever told Trump to call on that red-headed Russian girl in the audience was likely setting Trump up on behalf of the FBI. Go back and read my deconstruction of that history, including the possibility that USG knew all about Maria from March 2015 and began the scheme then. In July of 2015 Trump calls on Maria in an audience of 2,000 people in Las Vegas. If he did it because he was prompted to do it, then I would strongly suspect that whoever was close enough to

Trump to prompt him to do that was someone with ties to the Deep State and was (wittingly or unwittingly) used by them to get Trump to call on Maria to give carbonation to the "Can-O'-Russia-Scandal" that was already in the works. They wanted the video of Trump interacting with Maria for the day down the road that they cracked open their "Can-O'-Russia-Scandal."

Someone must ask Trump: Who told you to call on Maria in the audience?

A fifth thing to know is that the intermediary between William Barr and myself was also a friend of Steve Bannon. Before that intermediary died in that plane crash, he told me three things about Barr and Bannon.

One was that he had been in the White House the day AG Session's resigned. My friend had been in the office as the question of his successor was being discussed. That intermediary excused himself, walked out to the lawn, and called his mentor, William Barr. Asked if Barr would be interested in seeing his name being thrown in the hat. Barr thought for ten seconds, then said, "I'll do it. But only because I want to come in and burn the agency system down. The agencies have taken over DC." My friend went back into the West Wing and threw Barr's name into the hat in the room it was being discussed. Barr was chosen days later.

The second thing he told me: by 2020 Steve Bannon was jealous of me. In the White House he had learned about my alternative life in service to the United States and was green with envy: "Bannon always dreamed of being James Bond," my friend said.

The third thing my friend told me was something unsavory about Steve Bannon's personal life, and how it had once created an issue that this friend of mine had to fix. It is likely that Bannon worries that I know about it.

Whatever the reason, I can promise you that since at least October 2, 2020, the day that I called the DOJ and let them know I was about to go public with the material you have been learning about in this interview, Steve Bannon has done everything within his power to prevent anyone in media from talking to me. Every time I do a deposition these days, it always ends with a lawyer pulling out emails from Steve Bannon telling someone not to talk to me, not to listen to me, *Patrick Byrne is crazy*, things like that. Every deposition, they show me his emails to different people telling them that.

Since October 2020, it seems Steve has really bent over backwards to try to keep people from listening to what I have to say. Seems like a strange hobby.

Connect those dots as you wish. You've exhausted my knowledge of Steve Bannon.

Why didn't you come forward about all of this while Trump was still in office?

Well in a way I did, but unbelievably to me now, I still did not really grasp the depths of the corruption and kept getting tricked into remaining silent. Let me explain.

Remember, since 2015 I had been the one trying to convince the agencies that "there's some Russian operation going on here." I was frustrated, and thought that someday I would be sitting in front of a Senate panel talking about how our National Security Community had missed obvious indications of it, like Maria and things she told me. And with all the noise out of Washington in 2017, I was thinking that there must indeed be some Russian network that was going to get exposed, some Anna-Chapman event where the FBI swoops in and rounds up a dozen Russian sleepers across the USA. I was prepared for that and wondered if my little Russian grad student would turn out to be connected to it, or aware of it, or simply suspicious like I was that something like that was going on.

Once Trump got elected, I made a gameplan. My instinct was to go to the new authorities and fill them in, but I was worried that if I did, people might accuse me of misusing the relationship I had with the USG in order to affect domestic politics. I also thought I might get a tap on the shoulder from investigators within weeks of Trump's inauguration. In addition, my handler was replaced, and my new handler told me, *You were put through a lot of craziness over the last couple of years. Everything is being worked out with the DOJ, everything that needs to be communicated is being communicated.* That mollified me, but I was not sure I was doing the right thing by not calling anyone.

So, in the end, I adopted this strategy: *I will trust their claim they are talking to DOJ and everything has been cleared up with them by my handlers, and thus I will sit quiet for now. But if and when I get a tap on the shoulder from an investigator, I will tell everything. This strategy will absolve me of guilt in the face of any accusations that I was using knowledge gained through my avocation to affect domestic politics. In the meantime (and this is crucial), I will keep my eyes off the news regarding Russia matters swirling around DC, in order to keep my own memories pure.*

I thought that within weeks, a month or two at the outside, I would get that tap.

So 2017 kicked along like that. I played along with my instructions, but still waited for that tap-on-shoulder, and still kept my eyes off the news on the subject, so that my own memories could be 100 percent pure. Weeks turned into months. By about November 2017, the Russian stuff swirling in Washington solidified as the Mueller commission: again, I thought I would be contacted by them within days of their formation. Nothing. And again, I thought that there must indeed be some Anna Chapman-like network of Russian sleeper cells that Mueller was getting to the bottom of, and I was curious to see if and how Maria had been attached to it. Or aware of it. Or just suspicious of one existing, like me.

General H. R. McMaster, the National Security Advisor, sent me an invitation to lunch privately with him at the White House in the days before Christmas 2017. HR and I knew each other previously, for about a decade, from the days of the Iraqi surge. He never made clear to me if he knew precisely the nature of my relationship to the USG, but we had several mutual friends who were aware of it, so I thought he likely did.

At the end of our meeting, it was around December 20, 2017, we were back in his office after eating at the White House mess. At the last minute, just as I was getting up to put on my jacket, he asked, "What do you think of this crazy Russian stuff going on?"

It remains one of the regrets of my life that I looked at the time, saw I had only a minute, and decided, I am in a White House under federal investigation. As the Arabs say, "I cannot tell whose dick is in whose ass around here." I don't know which end is up. I will tell any investigator who comes to me what is going on, but should I just be blurting it out here within the White House to HR McMaster?

And just like that, I hesitated long enough that HR shrugged and dropped the question.

So I shrugged it off as well and left.

Some days I kick myself, thinking I may have saved the country all the trouble it is going through. On the other hand, others have told me that if I had tried to explain it to McMaster, he would have brought in the White House General Counsel's office, they would have gone directly back to the FBI and Deep State … and I would have been killed. As my handlers had warned.

So that gets us into 2018. I kept silent but waited for some investigator's tap-on-shoulder that never came. Not even with the Mueller matter in full swing. And still, I was being assured by my handlers that everything had all been conveyed to the DOJ anyway.

By Spring 2018 the flame on the Russian matter was getting so hot there was no way I could keep ignoring it. In May 2018 I decided, *I am going to drop my embargo on news about the Russian Investigation, I will bone up on it and figure out what is going on for myself.*

I studied the news over a few weeks in May and began having a terrible thought: What if this crazy Russian scandal that is consuming my country turns out not to be some Anna-Chapman-like network of Russian spies across America? Is there any chance the whole thing is going to turn out to be about… my little Russian grad student? The one I had an eight-month affair from July 2015–March 2016 trying to get FBI to heed, and they seemed to be deliberately ignoring…? Could that be?

I obsessively tried to fit together pieces that seem obvious now. Finally in June 2018 I went and sought out a certain Republican lawyer in DC, an extremely prominent one, perhaps the *most* prominent one in DC. I found him at a cocktail party and told him I had information on a bunch of dirty stuff including the truth about the Russia investigation and needed his help to go find the right person to talk to in the US Government. Practically rubbing his hands together in glee, he excitedly told me to come to his office the next morning and he would clear his schedule for it.

I showed up the next morning and began to walk him through the story. I got five minutes into it before he interrupted me to say, "I can tell you right now I'm not taking you to see *anyone*. Are you out of your mind? What you are going to do is you are going to go home, you're going to shut your mouth, and you're not going to say *anything* to *anyone* about this. If you open your mouth you are going to spend the rest of your life in prison. You are out of your mind if you think you are going to talk to anyone about this."

I told him that the correct analysis was not what was best for me as his client, but what the country needed. He told me as a lawyer he could not analyze it that way.

Then around July 8, 2018, I was in Atlantic City giving a talk on blockchain. When I caught up on the news that night, I discovered some FBI officials had been before Congress that day. The names were Strzock, Carlin, Priestap, McCabe, Comey. Other than Comey I had never previously heard any of the names. But I saw the videos of Congress ripping them apart, and I was horrified at their testimony. Clearly these FBI officials had been using their offices to conduct political espionage and shape domestic political events. Third World stuff.

Only after I formed that judgement did I notice in their testimony mention of their job titles: head of Counterespionage, head of Counter-Intelligence, chief of National Security Division, Executive Assistant Director, Director Comey. Get it?

Yes. Those were the titles in your chain of command on the Maria assignment?

Exactly. There in an Atlantic City hotel at 3:00 a.m. I put everything together. The dirty officials whose testimony that day I was watching on my iPad, who had clearly misused their positions to shape domestic politics… was in fact my chain of command. They were the guys who three years earlier had started giving me orders about Maria that had never made sense, and the instructions on the Hillary Clinton bribery two-and-a-half years previously.

There at 3:00 a.m. in Atlantic City, I decided to spill the beans. I had a choice: either go to NYC to spill the beans on Fox News (which would have me on anytime) or go to DC to spill the beans to someone in authority. At any other time in my life I would have done the hot-headed thing, gone on Fox, and launched into my story. But I thought, "I am always accused of being impulsive. For the first time in my life I am going to play this straight. I will go to DC and work with powers-that-be to straighten this out." I confess that a small part of my decision was avoidance-behavior: the thought of just going on TV and breaking my oath, my security clearance, and coming clean about what I knew was a lot to contemplate.

So I would go through channels in DC. But what channel would that be?

The next morning at 6:00 a.m. I was on a private jet to DC, doing my research from the plane. Let me explain that the thought of actually coming clean and opening up about this stuff is much more difficult than you might imagine. I had been sworn to secrecy countless times, I had a high-level security clearance. In addition, I had signed documents that promised me fifteen years if I ever opened my mouth, but the fear of prosecution did not matter much. Instead, I found that psychologically it was extremely difficult to contemplate, like being a Mob enforcer contemplating betraying his Family.

I thought of going to the Senate Judiciary, who had sent me on my quest all those years ago, but I saw that Lindsey Graham was the Ranking Republican. Enough said.

I reasoned as follows: the Constitution puts the power to declare war with the House, "the chamber closest to the people." I realized that it was not just that a couple dirty orders had been sent down my chain of command, but that the whole thing was worm-eaten. We were living through a soft-*coup*. This was national security, maybe national existence. I would go to the People's chamber and find the right guy.

That is how I zeroed in on House Member John Ratclife, a former federal prosecutor in terrorism-related matters who had become a Texas Congressman and was then sitting on Nunes's committee. In my experience, people in government who deal with terrorism are the most serious people of all within the USG. So I made a call and quickly got an appointment to see him for an hour, in a SCIF ("Secure Compartmentalized Information Facility"), that is, a special room where classified matters can be discussed. Congressman Ratcliffe showed up with the chief investigator for that Nunes committee, a former Army SOCOM officer.

Knowing that my story was an extremely complicated one, let alone one that would sound bat-shit crazy to people who knew me only as the CEO of a $2 billion public company, I decided to give them just bite-size pieces to digest. First, speaking to the retired SOCOM colonel, I established my bona fides by naming people that I knew he must know: when he acknowledged them, I told him to contact them, and they could confirm that I indeed had the relationship with USG I was claiming.

Then I told them of Hillary bribery. To give you a sense of how guarded I was, I told them only it had come from a country in Eurasia but did not mention Azerbaijan specifically.

The two men listened to me for an hour, conferred, then told me there were subpoenas going out in a few weeks and they would put my name at the top of the list, and have me come in to speak before a Congressional hearing in early September 2018, about six weeks away.

As we rose to leave, I made a prediction. I said, "A couple months ago there was an article in the *Daily Beast* about Maria Butina, a Russian grad student in town, a red-headed intellectual swanking around DC. Ring a bell?" They both looked at each other, momentarily perplexed, and then both acknowledged that they remembered the article.

I said, "If I am correct, you will see Maria emerge as a central figure in this Russian thing. If she does, it is all a hoax. I met her three years ago, reported her immediately, they have been following her from the day she arrived. I thought some Anna-Chapman-network was going to get uncovered, but now suspect they are constructing this all around her."

They both nodded their understanding, we shook hands, and parted.

I believe that was a Thursday. The following Tuesday morning, that CNN van with its FBI SWAT truck behind it arrived at Maria's apartment and arrested her.

So, I knew, Ratcliffe has to see I know what I am talking about.

A few weeks later, word leaked of a fresh round of subpoenas sent out from Congress. I waited, but mine never arrived in August. I waited through September, October…

Finally at the end of October one of my handlers met with me and in the course of a conversation about other matters said, "Patrick, you need to know that there are billionaires walking around this planet that we made, and we are prepared to do the same for you… you just have to stay calm and quiet through the election."

I did not know if he meant the one a week away, or the one in two years (2020), but in either case my one and only thought was, *I caught you now you* motherfuckers. *I got you! I looked for you since 2006, I found you, and I am going to rip your throat out.*

The next day I went back to DC to meet with Ratcliffe and his SOCOM guy again.

When they marched into the SCIF the first thing they said was, "After we met you last time, Maria Butina was arrested, so we knew you are not just crazy. And we were able to confirm about 25 percent of what you told us about your relationship to the government, but the rest is a black hole to us. There is a stonewall on information about you."

I asked, "I never got the subpoena you promised? Why not?"

They told me that once Maria had been arrested, the fact that there was an ongoing criminal matter to which I was a witness meant they were not able to send me a subpoena.

I actually exploded at them a bit. They had let months slip by because of some bureaucrat rules?

This time I had brought more evidence and gave them "Azerbaijan" for the first time.

I told them that if they were not moving, I was going public without them. Ratcliffe pointed out that it would do no good. There was no functioning rule of law in the nation, he said. AG Sessions had resigned a week or two previously, and no new Attorney General had been appointed. However, I had heard (and Congressman Ratcliffe confirmed) that he himself was under consideration to be appointed the new Attorney General. He counseled me, *Just stay quiet, the new appointment would be made, and if it were Ratcliffe, then he would hit the new job running because I had already brought him up to speed on everything.*

We parted on that pledge to each other.

Three months later, February 14, Valentine's Day, 2019, Barr was sworn in as AG.

In March I went back to see Congressman Ratcliffe. He had reviewed all my additional evidence and now understood the whole story that I have shared here. He asked if I was willing to begin talking and I told him that I was.

He brought in Senator Mike Lee. Mike and I knew each other from Utah. I explained a concise version of the story: setting up the Russian Hoax, bribing and blackmailing Hillary Clinton, the original Senate Judiciary Committee request, putting my chain of command in the position of having to sign off on an aggravated rape and murder if they wanted to continue their *coup*, them falling for it.

Senator Lee shook his head in bewilderment. He said, "Patrick, the Senate Judiciary Committee doesn't have the authority to do anything like this. Did they cite any statute?"

I said, "Senator, I don't do law, I do philosophy. *Federalist 51.*"

Mike Lee took me to the Senate Judiciary staffers, who were three generations past the ones I had known in 2005-2006. I walked them through everything. They were ashen, naturally. The lead investigator, Zachary, said, "There is no such thing as a letter such as you describe. But even if there were… Don't you think you took things a little far?"

I said, "Sir there is indeed such a letter, look in your files and it says that I get 'extraordinary latitude under the laws of the United States' to pursue my activities."

He said, "OK, but rape-and-murder? Tricking the directors of the FBI and CIA to sign off on rape and murder? Isn't that a little extreme?"

I replied, "Specter and Hatch both told me that they selected me because they heard I did 'extreme things to accomplish whatever I was asked to accomplish.'"

Days later I received a call: "Mr. Byrne, we're terribly embarrassed to say this…. But we checked our files from 2006 and we found a letter concerning you… and it says pretty much exactly what you say it says. We've never seen anything like this, we had no idea…!"

Arrangements were set in motion for me to get in front of Barr.

It took until April 5 to get in front of Barr. You know the story from there. I spoke with his people; they arranged a debriefing for me with FBI Office of Professional Responsibility. It was for a couple weeks later, the day after Maria's sentencing. I thought that seemed odd: since in that first DOJ meeting April 6, I had told them not only of bribing Hillary, but of the events surrounding Maria, shouldn't they debrief me fully before she was sentenced?

Anyway, a day or so after she was sentenced, I met with FBI Office of Professional Responsibility at a senior level. Two mature agents, sharp as tacks, debriefed me for hours. After several minutes, the lead agent said, "We'll let you keep running through this now, but you and I are going to be spending at least a couple weeks going through this in detail." But afterwards, he bounced that next meeting to the following Monday, then a week, then told me that a new commission was being formed (Durham) who would handle it all. Then… silence.

So around June 24, 2019, I went to see my rabbi in Omaha. That is the time I told you about, where he listened for twenty minutes, jumped up and paced, and told me I had to go public no matter the repercussions to myself. I told him that if I went public there were heads in DC that were going to explode. He said, "You let people in DC do *their* job; you do *your* job. You're a citizen, your country is burning, *your* job is to go public about all of this."

Did you love Maria Butina?

Well to some degree, that quote about a philosopher in love being like "a Cyclops with tiny, delicate hands" is true. So it was never really a question of love.

You can certainly say that I was quite fond of her. I felt tremendous admiration for her. I think she is extraordinary: brilliant, athletic, liberty minded. Selected for a boarding school for the most mentally and physically elite .0001 percent of Russian children, and a decade later graduates #2. Can talk Austrian Economics like Ron Paul. So smart and well-read that when she, at 26 years old, sat with me describing her aspiration to be president of Russia, it did not seem strange at all. It also did not seem strange to learn that at 93 General Mikhail Kalashnikov chose her, branded her with his name, at 23. I've been around some good universities, known some smart kids, I've even taught a few smart kids here and there... Maria is remarkable.

At no point did Maria or I think in terms of, "We should be together." We admired each other and were grateful to spend time together, her Mikhail Kalashnikov's girl, me Milton Friedman's guy, me wanting to see her on her way to be president of Russia. Believe me, Russia could do far worse. In fact, Russia has done far worse for about six hundred years.

But in 2006, as delusional as it sounds, 300 million Americans elected a Senate, which chose a Senate Judiciary Committee, which chose a chairman. He and half a dozen of his colleagues from both sides of the aisle as well as the Chairman of the Senate Intelligence Committee told me their power transcended every power within the United States, "systemic corruption was infiltrating the federal institutions of our nation's government," and they tasked me with disrupting it. Maria represented the perfect opportunity to do that.

At one point, an article appeared in *Daily Beast*[8] about a Russian grad student swanking around with big shots in DC. I told Maria that she is what is known as 'a loose end', and I tried to get Maria to walk over to the FBI, declare herself, and say, "You may have read things about me being here and have concerns. May I answer any questions that you have?" I never revealed to her more than that. I told her she did not have to be disloyal to Russia, but since her name was in the papers, she should clear up any misunderstandings with the FBI before they got out of hand.

She told me that as a loyal Russian she could never do it.

For what it's worth, I did try to make use of Maria in a way that would help her achieve her goals. I thought that, like Anna Chapman, she might spend a couple nights in jail, maybe a week, then would go back to Russia a national hero. On her way to the Duma. I had everything correct but the "couple nights in jail," which proved to be eighteen months in a box.

There is a movie I thought of as I was doing this, an under-appreciated movie called *Mad Dog & Glory* with Robert De Niro, Bill Murray, and Uma Thurman. De Niro is a wimpy police photographer, so wimpy the cops call him "Mad Dog" with irony. In a liquor store shootout, he saves the life of a civilian, Bill Murray, who turns out to be a gangster. In gratitude, Murray befriends De Niro, telling De Niro he wants to be the "facilitator of all your dreams." In time, De Niro confesses his dream was to be a tough guy, fighting bad guys, saving the girl. Instead, he is a wimpy police photographer.

In gratitude for saving his life, Gangster Bill Murray loans De Niro one of his girls, Uma Thurman. De Niro falls in love, naturally. Murray

---

8. "The Kremlin and GOP Have a New Friend – and Boy Does She love Guns"
https://www.thedailybeast.com/the-kremlin-and-gop-have-a-new-friendand-boy-does-she-love-guns

and De Niro continue being friends but eventually Bill Murray gets oddly rude, causing De Niro to pull away. So Bill Murray lets De Niro know he is coming to take the girl back. De Niro must—you guessed it—be a tough guy, fight the bad guy, and save the girl. Murray is beaten, but as he withdraws, he mumbles to De Niro, "… the facilitator of all your dreams, pal." It's subtle, but the meaning is: it was all setup by Bill Murray to turn De Niro into what he dreamed of being. That is how he repaid De Niro for saving him in the robbery: by creating the scenario that gave De Niro the opportunity to be who he dreamed of being. I think people missed what a smart movie it was.

When Maria got back in Russia, I sent her that movie. She understood what I was saying, of course. She is *so* clever.

I am not sure it took the sting off eighteen months in a windowless box the size of my shower stall, but she has forgiven me for setting her up. If I understand correctly, in her months in a box she became something of a Christian. "Ballad of Reading Gaol," right?

I have pointed out to her an irony. When we met, we discussed how within Russian Orthodoxy there is the belief that the salvation of mankind is purchased through the capacity of Russian people to endure immiseration and suffering. I pointed out to her that perhaps it will be through Maria's suffering, that the ultimate exposure of the American Deep State becomes possible, and with that, the chances for world peace will go up dramatically.

Just to be clear, and since the Russian press has reported it anyway, when she got out of her windowless box and back to Moscow, I sent her $1 million in Bitcoin. The Russian Communist Party (which hates her—she's their Ron Paul) made a fuss about it, acting like it means I control her. No, Maria and I barely stay in contact: I did it thinking it was just the American Good Guy thing to do. After all, at the deepest level it was *my* scheme, which just played out a little farther than I had planned. Barr's DOJ had a snit about me sending $1 million of Bitcoin to Maria, but I let them know, *If there is one subject about which the USG can keep its opinions to itself with me, it is on the subject of my ethical duty to Maria Butina.* I also got her to sign a piece of paper that she would never sue me or the DOJ for setting her up and putting her in a windowless box for eighteen months, and DOJ was mollified by that.

That was generous. Still, for a man who claims he admired Maria Butina, you misused her horribly.

Oh yes. I have noticed that it takes a while, but when people understand the whole story, they come to see it from this angle. I am surprised it took you so long. Yes, absolutely, I make no pretense about it. I'm one of several villains here. No doubt. She's a wonderful woman, and I misused her terribly in a scheme of my own. Guilty as charged.

Yes, you did. But...you respected and cared about Maria, clearly. "Deeply fond" of her, you said? Maybe you loved her but won't say. But you at least cared for her a lot. Right? You wanted to help her become President of Russia, right?

Yes.

Yet you fed her to the Deep State like a mouthguard into boiling water, to see what dental imprints the Deep State would make on her. Did I hear that correctly?

Yes. Guilty as charged.

Do you see anything contradictory there? Who would do something like that?

[Byrne stares into the woods, perhaps thinking of the decades that separate him from his teenage self that ran these trails. Only after a long silence does Byrne answer.]

I suppose Arlen Specter didn't pick my name out of a hat.

It is the end of our last conversation with Byrne. After our long walk we have arrived back at our cars, and we drive in separate directions.

Byrne with his brother Mark James Byrne (RIP)
Ft. Wayne, Indiana, 1964

POSTSCRIPT

In late 2023 I met a well-known Washington, DC figure for the first time. He had read an abridged version of this interview in the launch of *Capital Times Magazine*. He cleared up one mystery. He told me that in 2015 – 2016 the *Washington Times* was organizing a weekly luncheon with politicians and other press. In February 2015, Maria Butina had shown up at that luncheon (she was visiting DC for the first time, as I mentioned in the story you just read). In this DC think-tank's luncheon, she was professional and polite, raised her hand and asked questions, and when the meeting was over networked among those in attendance. Afterwards, the man organizer discussed with his staff the Russian redhead who had been so prominent in the luncheon. He told them not to let Maria into the following weekly luncheon, as he did not want a good-looking Russian gal there raising eyebrows and making people uncomfortable.

The next day this man received a phone call from FBI Special Agent Peter Strzok. Agent Strzock requested that Maria not be blocked from luncheons, that the Bureau would prefer he let her continue attending and that they would be keeping an eye on her.

The man in question ignored the FBI request and kept Maria out of subsequent luncheons on the grounds that it would make the other guests more comfortable.

In the story above I claimed that I was *sure* the FBI knew about and were on top of Maria by July 2015 (as soon as I reported her), but I *speculated* that she may have been noticed on her February–March 2015 visit and the scheme cooked up after she her departed. The truth is even worse: by March 2015, the FBI not only *knew* about Maria, they were *already* greasing the skids for her to network around DC.

This new information collapses the waveform: the truth is not simply that Maria was *noticed* on that her visit to Washington in early 2015; it is that the Russian Collusion setup was already in *operation* by that month. Which, I note again, was three months before Donald Trump declared his candidacy.

Which is one further devastating proof point that the Russian Collusion matter had nothing to do with Trump: it was planned, set-up, and was being executed against the Republican Party by our National Security apparatus by March 2015, three months before Trump came down an escalator.

Patrick M. Byrne
Milan, Italy
December 6, 2023

Made in the USA
Coppell, TX
12 June 2024

33411038R00105